COMPETITIVE
SELLING

COMPETITIVE SELLING

OUT-PLAN
OUT-THINK
OUT-SELL
TO WIN EVERY TIME

LANDY CHASE

New York   Chicago   San Francisco   Lisbon   London
Madrid   Mexico City   Milan   New Delhi   San Juan
Seoul   Singapore   Sydney   Toronto

The **McGraw·Hill** Companies

1 2 3 4 5 6 7 8 9 10 DOC/DOC 1 5 4 3 2 1 0

ISBN   978-0-07-173889-7
MHID   0-07-173889-4

McGraw-Hill books are available at special quantity discounts to use as premiums and sales promotions or for use in corporate training programs. To contact a representative, please e-mail us at bulksales@mcgraw-hill.com.

CONTENTS

ACKNOWLEDGMENTS

The Roman philosopher Seneca is credited with the observation that "Luck is where preparation meets opportunity." I consider myself lucky to have crossed paths in life with a number of people who gave me opportunities in various ways to benefit from my efforts at preparation. Thus I would like to say "thank you" to

The Citadel, for teaching me the value of persistence in the face of adversity.

Jim Poss, for mentoring me as my first sales manager.

Mitchell Touart, for being a role model for me as an up-and-coming salesperson.

Norm McCarty, for helping me to become a corporate sales trainer.

Jim Cook, for leadership by example and for sharing with me the power of the Blind Hog Theorem.

Greg Roth, for being my first client and providing me the opportunity to launch my business.

Regina Landry, our marketing director, for your loyalty and your superb ability to take care of the needs of our clients.

The editing and production staff at McGraw-Hill, for your collaboration and partnership in producing this work.

Jim Currow, for your loyalty, business, collaboration, and friendship.

Zig Ziglar, for being a role model for the speaking profession, and for your unique ability to make everyone you come into contact with feel important.

My parents, for teaching me the importance of being nice to other people.

To my family, for your support and patience during the writing of this book.

INTRODUCTION
The Dominant Predator

In business, as in life, we often gain the most from our greatest failures. The selling methods outlined in this book are born of one such failure, a humbling experience that I had years ago, when I was preoccupied with starting my business and momentarily took my eye off the ball. And so I begin with the story of a competitive sale—and the worst presentation that I ever made in 25 years of professional selling.

Like most competitive selling situations, this opportunity began as a call-in lead. A large firm in Atlanta, Georgia, had decided to find an outside resource to develop a sales training program. The call came because the firm was referred by a client of mine, and my company was one of several being invited to participate. After the usual niceties, my contact got down to business.

"Okay—here's the deal. We have a meeting at our corporate offices here in Atlanta on the morning of February 4. I am forwarding a 'Summary of Requirements' so that you can prepare your presentation. We would like for you to come in on that date, at 8:30 in the morning, to show us what you have. You will be allowed 30 minutes. You will be preceded and followed by two competitors. Would you like to participate?"

"Absolutely," I replied. "Who else besides you will be at your meeting?"

The person contacting me was not the decision maker—an all-too-common trait of call-in leads. "It will be me and three other people" was his reply.

"Wonderful. I look forward to seeing you then."

And that was it. I didn't ask who my competitors were. I didn't ask about the other people involved in the buying decision or what their roles were. I didn't ask to have access to those people. In fact, I didn't ask for any of the lessons covered in this book. Instead, I reviewed the "Summary of Requirements" like many sales pros would. I prepared my recommendations per the request for proposal (RFP), and on the appointed day, I went to Atlanta. I was ready at 8:30 that morning for my presentation meeting with the four-person committee.

Except there was no meeting with a four-person committee. When I walked into their boardroom that morning, 22 people sat around a large conference table, silently watching me. Twenty-two people—and I had no idea who they were, why they were there, why I was there, what they expected from me, or what I was supposed to do. We stared blankly at one another for a moment. This moment, as it turns out, was the high point of my presentation—it was all downhill from there.

I began by reviewing the list of items that my contact had provided for my preparation. "It is my understanding that you are looking for...." I went down the list until I finished the review. I looked up then and asked whether I'd missed anything.

Silence. I watched several of the participants look at each other, puzzled. I saw a woman to my right scratching her head. Someone coughed. A man in the back of the room crossed his arms and scowled at me. I then came to the realization that I had made a terrible mistake and was now paying for it. I was in the middle of a complete, disastrous melt-down.

There was a flipchart and markers next to me, so I picked up a marker. I began drawing a concept from my proposal on the flipchart. This tactic, predictably, went nowhere. Now there was another period of silence. I remembered that I had brought five sets of my boilerplate marketing materials with me. I distributed them to the conference table. "Would the five of you mind sharing this?" I asked the first group of people I came to. The five of them agreed to do so, probably out of pity. Comparatively speaking, this tactic actually went fairly well; afterward, a person to my left *did* whisper to his peer, "He made a remarkable recovery!" My time, mercifully, was up at this point.

I didn't bother following up, but I did learn later that one of my competitors did not make the same mistakes that I made. He was a *dominant predator*; he knew how to win at competitive sales. He'd done his homework and successfully talked to most of the people in that room before making his appearance that morning. Then he delivered a customized proposal that met everyone's needs and expectations. His presentation cleaned my clock. He got the account, whereas I got a good spanking—one that I had coming to me.

Since that day, I have worked with tens of thousands of salespeople in over 60 different industries. All of them, like you and me, compete for business on a daily basis. A select few, however, are *dominant predators*—salespeople who consistently win business, at higher prices, against their competition. In this book you will find some of their best techniques, some modified and improved on, as well as a number of my own successful strategies to create a blueprint for your success in winning competitive selling opportunities.

Today, I win the vast majority of competitive sales in which I find myself participating, to the extent that my peers in the speaking business who lose business to me tease me, good-naturedly, about it. What this book offers you is a proven, step-by-step process on how to win—consistently—against your competition. It will provide you with everything you need to become a dominant predator. It has worked for me, and it will work for you.

Today's buyers shop around for everything; selling now occurs in a business environment where you are almost never the only vendor being considered. Customers have learned that they benefit by having different options compete against each other. So it follows that we who sell also must learn some new strategies. We must upgrade our skills in dealing with savvy, educated buyers. And if we must compete for business, we must compete with the utmost in skill—because skill, not what we are selling, is what makes or breaks competitive sales.

A common misconception about dominant predators is that they win sales by competing with other sellers. The reality is that they win because they compete with themselves. They realize that the key to winning competitive sales is all about skill within the buying process, not about which competitors are involved. They then develop skill strategies designed to give them an advantage over their competition.

This book, in essence, is the consummate advantage. Following the natural progression of the competitive selling cycle from start to finish, you will learn how to

- Position yourself as the best-qualified expert to meet your client's current needs and conditions
- Differentiate your value proposition from that of your competition so that there is no issue of "apples to apples" when it comes to your recommendations
- Identify your opening position and establish your strategy in the competitive sale before ever setting foot in the buyer's place of business
- Identify all the key players in the competitive sale and get access to these people before you move to a proposal

- Conduct a needs analysis that will serve to make your proposal more appropriate, more customized, and more comprehensive than anything your competitors can offer
- Identify and get access to the one person who controls the decision
- Handle and disarm political issues with skill and professionalism
- Eliminate competitors from consideration without bad-mouthing them
- Sell winning proposals that ignore stated budgets
- Negotiate effectively when selling against other competitors
- Close sales that lock out competitors and win you the business

Key ideas throughout the book are appropriately notated as Predator Points—these are the most important principles in the process. Learn them. Use them.

I am not going to tell you that by reading this book you will win every single competitive sale that comes your way. After all, you cannot control all the variables in the competitive sale. However, you can control most of them. And by controlling most of the variables, you control your success and your destiny.

Chapter | 1

VALUE VERSUS PRICE

The *Real* Reason You Lose to Competition

You purchased this book because you are trying to figure out why you're losing sales to the competition. This book will provide the answers that you seek. However, to get the return on investment (ROI) that you expect from your purchase, you and I need to establish agreement on one key point before proceeding: You are not losing sales to your competitors because their price is lower than yours.

That assumption, while virtually universal in the arena of business-to-business (B2B) sales, is fundamentally flawed. It is a lame excuse that you can give to your boss if you wish, but it has no place here. In fact, if you believe that pricing plays a role in whether or not you win competitive sales, you should place this book back where you found it and get your money back immediately, for you are misdiagnosing the source of the problem. Until you accept this simple point about pricing for what it is, this book will not help you.

Still reading? Then keep an open mind, and I'll prove my point in the following scenario.

Let's Role-Play

In this exercise I will be your potential customer, and you will play the role of the salesperson. Here is the scenario: I am currently in the market for what you provide, and I have called you in to discuss my wants and needs. You are now at my office. Incidentally, I also have made an identical call to one of your competitors, with whom I will be meeting at a later time. I have not shared this information with you.

You and I now have our initial sit-down to discuss my needs and your capabilities. We have a positive initial meeting, and you handle the discussion well. You ask a number of questions about my business, and I provide you with answers to your questions. You then give me an overview of your company's capabilities, and as a result of this overview, I am interested in what you can offer. We conclude our meeting by agreeing that you will return to your office and prepare a proposal for me and schedule a second meeting to review your formal recommendations at a later time.

Fast-forward to the next day: I am now meeting with your competitor. My meeting with her is very similar to the one that I had with you; she asks a lot of the same questions that you did, and she, too, provides me with an overview of her company's capabilities. As was the case with you, I am interested in a proposal from her. We conclude by agreeing that she will prepare a proposal for me, and I schedule her second visit to do this, just as I did with you.

Following these initial meetings, both of you submit your proposals to me. Both proposals are well designed, but both, as expected, are similar in their content and recommendations. After all, the question-and-answer portions of each meeting were very similar. You both asked similar questions, and to each of you I gave similar answers.

There is one notable difference, however, in the two proposals. Your recommendations are similar, yes, but—surprise!—your competitor's price is lower than yours.

Finally, my decision: After weighing both proposals and your respective recommendations, I elect, in this case, to buy from your lower-cost competitor.

In other words, you lost on price, right?

If you are like the vast majority of the salespeople with whom I have worked over the years, you would agree. To which I would reply that you don't understand the nature of the problem you face, nor do you have an accurate grasp of why you lost the business. The difference in pricing had absolutely nothing whatsoever to do with why you lost this sale, and until you understand and accept this point, you will never win consistently against your competition.

PREDATOR POINT

If your buyer has the financial ability to pay for your offering, price is eliminated as a reason for losing to a competitor.

Why Did You Really Lose the Sale?

So it wasn't the money. What, then, cost you the opportunity?

Let's first address the issue of when it really *is* the money.

If I do not have adequate funds to buy from you—in other words, if I simply don't have the financial means to pay your fee, either out of pocket or through financing—then yes, that is a price problem. Of course, as I am sure you realize, such a situation is almost never the case.

However, if your buyer has the financial means to buy from you—and, let's face it, they almost always have that ability—this eliminates price as a reason for choosing your competitor. Put another way, if I have the money to buy from you but choose not to do so, then money is not the issue that is driving my buying decision.

So why did you lose this opportunity? You lost it because, after weighing both options, I did not see enough difference in value between your recommendation and your competitor's to warrant spending the additional money. This has nothing to do with your pricing. It has everything to do with your failure to differentiate your value proposition.

This is a problem, yes—but it is a correctable skill problem, and you can do something about it!

When selling against competition, your success depends entirely on your ability to *persuasively* demonstrate that what you have, in terms of value, is clearly superior to the other options being considered. Differentiating your recommendations from those of your competitors will result in consistent wins; failure to accomplish this results in what we just witnessed—an "apples-to-apples" competition in which all options being considered appear to offer the same thing. Absent a difference in value, pricing becomes a default position; it is the only point of reference available for separating one option from another. This is how the lowest-priced vendor becomes the most attractive one—not merely because the price was so attractive. Let's set aside your desire to win competitive sales for a moment and look at this situation from what matters—the buyer's perspective. We have an obligation to the potential customer to help him or her make a well-informed business decision. When a decision is made based on price, the decision is not a well-informed one, and we as sales people therefore have failed in our obligation to the potential customer. We have failed to educate the buyer on our value proposition—and we have paid a penalty for this failure.

Now that we understand the problem—and that it is *our* problem— what can we do about it? How, given the competitive nature of selling, do you separate yourself from all other options? How do you show a buyer—clearly and conclusively—that you are not like any of the other vendors being considered? This is both a challenge and an opportunity. To begin, let's look at what is meant by the term *value*.

PREDATOR POINT

Losing business to competitors is a correctable skill problem.

How Your Buyer Defines *Value*

When selling against competition, there are three fundamental areas in which you have the ability to differentiate your value proposition. These are

1. *You*—In other words, what you personally bring to the table as a value-added resource to your potential customer
2. *Your support team*—Meaning the personnel in your organization who provide training, technical service, and customer support following your sale
3. *Your deliverables*—The product or service that you are actually selling

Figure 1.1

The Three Levels of Value Differentiation.

Of these three areas, the one that offers you the *least* opportunity for differentiation is what you are selling—your deliverables. In other words, from the buyer's perspective, what you offer, be it a product or a service, is the most commoditized aspect of your value proposition. That is why it appears at the bottom of the figure.

The buyer's point of view, right or wrong, is that, with regard to what is being offered, he or she can choose any one of several options and be reasonably satisfied with the purchase. It does not matter whether this perception is accurate or not. If this is the buyer's perception, this becomes the buyer's reality.

Despite this point, the vast majority of salespeople will expend virtually all their time and effort discussing, promoting, and attempting to differentiate their product offering. By doing so, they completely miss the opportunity for differentiation. They waste their time and the buyer's time. They unintentionally ignore the decision factors that matter—those where real value differentiation can be demonstrated.

Thus the buyer's perception is that he or she can do business with any one of several options and be reasonably satisfied. On such a level playing field, what does the buyer value above all else from you, the seller?

The Unpaid Consultant

In 25 years of selling, the worst advice for salespeople that I have ever heard was, ironically, the slogan of a firm that trains salespeople: "Don't be an unpaid consultant."

The logic here is that buyers will "use" you for free advice if you let them, and therefore you should refrain from providing them with such assistance.

This, in my opinion, is fundamentally flawed logic.

Buyers want to buy from people they view as experts. They wish to partner with salespeople who understand their issues and are capable of helping them run their businesses better. Sellers who can sell are a dime a dozen—but high-value *business advisors* are a rare, and sought-after, commodity.

Buyers ask for such advice only from people whom they deem worthy of providing it—meaning people who are viewed as experts. In fact, the highest compliment that a potential customer can pay you is to ask for your advice when they are not buying anything. When they do this—when they think enough of your expertise to ask for your opinion—you will own the account. They can get what you sell elsewhere, yes—but if they do that, they will not have you to work with any more.

The message? Strive every day to be the "unpaid consultant." Give freely of your opinion when asked for it. Seek opportunities to be the unpaid consultant. People want your opinion for a reason: They view you as an expert. Leverage this whenever possible. Make them depend on you, and they will swear loyalty to you.

A good example of this is the relationship that I have with my certified public accountant (CPA). My office is headquartered in North Carolina—a distance of over 500 miles from her office in Ohio. Despite the distance, for over a decade I have maintained a professional relationship with her firm, although I could easily find another local professional to provide the same basic services. In fact, there are dozens of people within a stone's throw of my office who do exactly the same kind of work.

Why, then, do I continue to send my financial data 500 miles away instead of working with someone locally? It certainly isn't for the basic services she provides: income statements, tax reporting, and bookkeeping. No, those are the commodities of her profession. It certainly isn't her fees either; my experience has been that they are higher than most people with whom she competes.

I work with her—or rather, she has my unwavering loyalty—because of what she doesn't charge for, but what is priceless to me nonetheless. Specifically:

- She understands my business.
- She understands how to apply her expertise to shore up one of my weaknesses (I'm a sales guy, not an accountant).
- She shows me how to use her expertise to run my business better.

In short, I can get what she does—accounting services—from virtually anyone, but then, if I did, I wouldn't have her to work with anymore. That one critical factor is why I would never, ever consider switching accountants. My relationship with her firm has evolved into one of *dependence*.

This relationship was put to the test unexpectedly a couple of years ago. I had received a form letter from her in the mail. She sent this announcement to all her clients, thanking us for our loyalty over the years—and politely informing us that owing to the demands created by the growth of her firm, she could no longer accommodate all of us. In other words, a few of us were going to have to go.

When I opened and read my copy of this letter, I was on the phone with her before the letter had a chance to float to my desk. When she answered my call, I begged. I pleaded. "Please, please, make me one of your keepers! I'm a simple business! I don't cause problems! I pay on time! Don't do this to me! Do it to someone else!" In other words, I, the customer, was in a complete panic.

Fortunately, I wasn't in danger; in fact, she found my reaction amusing. I wasn't laughing; I was desperate!

After I hung up the phone, I thought, "Wow! I'm the client, and here I am begging one of my vendors: Please keep selling to me."

That is what perceived expertise does for you. Do you have that kind of relationship with your customers? Do they depend on you for advice? If they do, you never have to worry about losing their business to your competition.

Are there implications for your expertise in the competitive selling environment—when selling to a new potential customer who is evaluating several options? To answer this question, I'll speak to you as a business owner who meets regularly with people just like you—and makes buying decisions every day, just like your potential customers do.

When you come to my office to meet with me, I know next to nothing about you. Would I be out of line to wonder what your personal qualifications are for partnering with me and my company? I am weighing several competitive options as part of my buying decision. Would not your professional credentials determine how much weight I give to the recommendations that you will be making?

Furthermore, when I first meet with you, isn't it true that all I really have to work from regarding first impressions is that you seem to be a nice person? Do you think that being "nice" is going to be enough to persuade me to buy from you instead of the other options?

Let's also assume here that you do, indeed, bring a wealth of experience and professional expertise within your industry to the table.

How, exactly, am I supposed to know that?

Now let's take a look at how to address these important points.

PREDATOR POINT

The highest compliment that a client can ever pay you is to request your opinion when they are not making a purchase.

How to Market Your Expertise

To establish your credibility with new buyers, you must document your professional credentials in the form of a *biography sheet*. This is a single-page document that summarizes, on one piece of paper, what your personal qualifications are for providing value to your prospective client. It shows that you are worthy of the term *advisor*. A sample biography sheet is provided in Figure 1.2.

As you can see, this document should be written in paragraph form and in the third person. It also—this is a requirement—must have your photograph. This is an item that some salespeople seem to have an issue with, so let's consider how another printed product makes good use of photography in achieving sales objectives. Consider *People* magazine.

People offers nothing that is going to affect the further development of your career. Get a life, people! Whether or not Jennifer and Angelina work out their differences over Brad does not affect the course of your life and success in any measurable way.

So why is *People* so popular? It succeeds because it focuses on two very basic human traits: (1) We are drawn to photos, and (2) we are naturally curious about other people. *People* uses a combination of flashy photography and meaningless gossip to draw readers. And it works! The people at *People* are very good at what they do, and they are therefore very successful.

These two principles apply to your biography sheet as well. To illustrate, put your thumb over the picture in the sample shown, and you will see that the document turns into a sheet of meaningless words. Now remove your thumb. With the photo, it becomes a completely different document, doesn't it? For this reason, having your photo on the page is an absolute requirement because it makes the person who sees it curious to read it. A color head-and-shoulders business photo is best for this purpose.

Figure 1.2

Sample biography sheet.

Figure 1.2 (*Continued*)

Sample biography sheet.

Josh Maret

Office Phone: 904-819-3579

Email:
Joshua.Maret@staugustine.com

The St. Augustine Record

Inside Digital Media Rep

Please contact me to
schedule a complimentary
digital media consultation

Let's Grow Your Business Together.

Josh specializes in helping local business owners to increase foot traffic and grow sales from a specific market by creating and implementing marketing strategies that are designed around the unique business needs of each advertiser.

Josh has focused exclusively on the St Augustine community and their classified, service directory and employment needs. After designing hundreds of ad programs, this market focus has provided him with a wealth of knowledge about what works – and what doesn't – when it comes to reaching a specific market.

He consistently gets results for his customers by evaluating each client's marketing challenges, and then designing an ad solution to reach the community in a cost effective way to attain a maximum return-on-investment.

These programs often include a combination of service directory advertising in the newspaper, special sections, and online listings as well as partnering with display ad reps to make display ads in the paper. Josh utilizes the unique marketing resources of The St Augustine Record to deliver high-value outcomes to retail advertisers, including:

- Targeting and attracting specific market demographics
- Increasing foot traffic to existing locations
- Successfully promoting sales and other special events
- Creating high attendance at store openings
- Increasing competitive market share
- Expanding geographic customer reaches within a specific market

Being a St Augustine native Josh has the knowledge and experience to help you in all of your business advertising and employment needs. His tailored approach and local knowledge makes him the perfect partner to help generate the much needed traffic your business deserves.

The St. Augustine Record

www.staugustine.com

YAHOO!

Figure 1.2 (*Continued*)

Sample biography sheet.

Partner With Me To Attract New Customers

David Sandeen
Multimedia Consultant,
Majors Advertising

David has almost 20 years of sales experience – 10 in advertising sales. He has served in multiple sales positions starting in retail sales, where he received Salesperson of the Year, as well as Salesperson of the Year for the entire advertising division. From there, David added national sales to his development and handled the telecommunication and travel categories with revenues of more than $8.5 million.

In 2006, David took on a new venture at the Times-Union and headed the new in-house agency, Blue Bridge Media. There, David worked to assist customers in all areas of sales and marketing.

Today, David works as a multimedia consultant in the majors adverting department and manages revenues more than $12 million annually. He works with the likes of Dillard's, JCPenney's and Wal-Mart and helps them develop plans and budgets to assist his clients achieve their goals.

David has been happily married for 12 years. When not working, he enjoys spending time with his three kids, coaching, mentoring and volunteering.

David

Office Phone: 904-359-4113

Cell Phone: 904-534-4308

Email: david.sandeen@jacksonville.com

The Florida Times-Union
WWW.JACKSONVILLE.COM

Figure 1.2 (*Continued*)

Sample biography sheet.

National Sales Trainer
LANDY CHASE
M.B.A. C.S.P.

Based in Charlotte, North Carolina, Landy Chase is a nationally active sales expert – one of a handful of speakers that specializes exclusively in sales force and sales management productivity. Since founding his company in 1993, he has given over two thousand paid presentations to corporate and association groups in over sixty different industries, with clients all over the U.S. as well as in Australia, Asia, Europe and South America. He has earned a reputation for delivering exceptionally high-value, practical content, skillfully blended with humor, relevant examples and personal stories.

As a speaker with a client re-hire rate in excess of ninety percent, Chase's personal qualifications rank at the very top of sales speakers nationally and include repeat national President's Club awards as a sales professional, formal experience as a National Sales Trainer for a two-billion-dollar service provider, and management experience directing the efforts of sales forces in both small business and major-account sales.

Chase is a graduate of The Citadel, The Military College of South Carolina, and earned his MBA from Xavier University. He holds the Certified Speaking Professional (CSP) designation from the National Speakers Association, the highest earned level of excellence in the industry and a distinction representing the top seven percent of all members of the speaking profession. An established author, he writes a sales column that is carried around the US by both newspapers and industry trade publications. His latest book, *Competitive Selling*, was published in hardcover world-wide by McGraw-Hill in July 2010.

❖ Keynotes
❖ Breakout Sessions
❖ Seminars
❖ Corporate Sales Meetings
❖ Sales Training Programs

For more information:
800.370.8026
www.landychase.com

The biography sheet concept also has great relevance for the other people in your company who provide value to the potential customer. Every competitor will claim to have outstanding people in customer service, technical support, training, accounting, etc. Well, who are those people? And more specifically, what makes your people better than those of the options that I am considering?

You already know that excellent service is a critical factor in buying decisions. To market your company's service capabilities, you must create biography sheets for every person who has potential customer contact. You must document everyone's expertise. You must be the one option to substantiate the claim that all competitors will make: "We have excellent people."

Using the Biography Sheet

Now that you understand the value of documenting expertise, the next question becomes how to use this tool as a competitive weapon. Two extremely effective uses of the biography sheet are as follows:

1. Every time that you prepare a formal proposal for a client, include the biography sheets of you and your support team in your proposal. Assuming that you have one, I recommend placing these in the left inside pocket of your proposal jacket. When you go over these in your presentation, say this to the prospective client:
   "If you make the decision to buy from our company, here are the people who will be responsible for ensuring your satisfaction."

2. As a habit, every single time that you set up an appointment with a new contact—be it at an existing account or at a prospective one—mail or e-mail your biography sheet, with a thank-you note attached, *prior* to the first meeting. Example:

"Dear Fred, Thank you for the opportunity to meet you on July 18. I'm looking forward to our meeting. Attached please find a brief summary of my qualifications for helping you with your needs."

Do you want to make an excellent first impression on a new contact *before* you ever meet with them? Do you want to establish, *up front,* that you are not the same as your competitors? Then follow this procedure every time you have a meeting with someone new—and watch what happens.

Letters of Recommendation

Infomercials on television have become a popular and highly effective way for marketers to introduce new products to consumers. They are also a very expensive advertising tool.

If you study the medium, you will notice that only about 20 percent of the air time used focuses on the product being offered. The other 80 percent consists of an endless parade of customers chirping happily about how pleased they have been with their purchase. Infomercial marketers do this because they understand the power of testimonials as an influence tool for driving sales. You should, too.

Potential customers perceive risk in buying from any vendor for the first time. When weighing competitive options, they will gravitate to the option that appears to offer the least amount of risk. Being perceived as the safer alternative—the one most likely to deliver as promised—is therefore an important aspect of winning competitive sales. Nothing is more effective in removing risk for your potential customer than the opportunity to examine the experience of your other potential customers. In the competitive selling environment, we don't need television to get this point across. We need documentation. We need *letters of recommendation.*

Most sellers will have, at most, two or three testimonial letters that they can produce on request. This is woefully inadequate. Is having two or three happy customers really enough documentation to demonstrate conclusively your ability to deliver value? Furthermore, can we safely assume that you competitors also can produce two or three similar letters from their best customers? If so, consider this: If I have two or three letters from your customers saying nice things about you and I have two or three letters from your competitor's customers saying nice things about your competitor, where, exactly, have you separated yourself?

To differentiate ourselves from competitors, we need, to use lawyer lingo, *a preponderance of the evidence.* To stand out, you must provide overwhelming, irrefutable evidence to the buyer that you are the risk-free choice—that you provide consistently outstanding value to your customers.

To meet this standard, you need, at a minimum, 12 to 15 letters of recommendation from satisfied customers. Furthermore, all your letters need to deliver one common message—results, which is the only thing that your customer cares about. Let's look at how to get to this number—quickly and easily.

Letters of recommendation are most effective when they meet the following three criteria:

- They describe an attained improvement, benefit, or result.
- They are signed by the client and are on the client's letterhead.
- They are less than two years old.

When asked, virtually all your satisfied customers will tell you that, yes, they would be delighted to write you a letter of this nature. Then you generally run into a little problem—actually getting the customer to write the letter. You can't really blame them because, for them, this is like "working for free". This is the reason why they rarely get around to doing it.

More important, most customers do not think in the same terms that you do. In other words, they are not likely to include the things in the letter that would matter to a prospective buyer. For example, they are likely to write you a letter that talks about how nice you are and what a fine company you are to deal with while completely overlooking the fact that your recommendations saved them over half a million dollars in the last calendar year.

What follows, then, is a three-step method that is (1) highly effective at getting excellent recommendation letters and (2) ensures that what needs to be said gets said—every time.

First, call your happy clients and "fish for compliments." Make this a customer-service call. Interview your customer on the telephone. Ask such questions as "What did you like the most about how we handled our most recent project together?" and "What were the net savings to your company?" and "How would you rate the technical expertise of our people against other vendors with whom you do business"?

While you are conducting this discussion, *write down your customer's comments*. The feedback to your questions will form the backbone of the letter, as you will see in a moment.

After collecting this feedback, ask the customer this question: "Would you be willing to give us a letter of recommendation that states what you just said?"

Remember, this is a satisfied customer; therefore, the vast majority will immediately say, "Of course."

Now take control of the process. Assume responsibility for getting the letter completed. Say this: "As a convenience to you, why don't I draft the letter for you? I'll e-mail it to you as a Word document, and when it is in a format that you like, just put it on your letterhead and send it back. How does that sound?"

Note the use of the word *draft* in the preceding statement. We didn't say, "Why don't I *write* the letter for you"; the word *draft* implies that the customer can change your wording. This is an important choice of words that makes a big difference in your success rate. Incidentally, satisfied customers almost never change anything in your draft, but it is important to make this offer.

You can expect the response, "That would be wonderful!" Most people will be absolutely delighted that you will take on this task for them because you are willing to do the work involved. Here is a real bonus: You ensure that all those wonderful things that the customer said in your phone interview appear in the letter. And because you are not embellishing or exaggerating, but merely quoting them, the great likelihood is that you will get back a letter that is the exact twin of the letter that you drafted.

Now That I Have Them—How Do I Use Them?

Once you have 12 to 15 recommendation letters, place them in a stapled packet with a cover sheet that reads, "Letters of Recommendation from Satisfied Clients." Make plenty of sets, and keep them in your office for use in competitive selling situations.

The best time to bring these out is at the end of your first meeting. Encourage your buyer to read them over, and encourage the buyer to contact anyone on your list for more information.

A final note: You might be concerned that your competitors could conceivably obtain this packet from one of your prospective buyers and begin attempting to sell to those customers. Yes, that could happen. So what? These are your best customers. Why do you care whether your competitors call on them or not? If your relationship with any of these accounts doesn't stand up to this point, they should not be asked to participate.

The List of References

A third and final persuasion tool that completes the *preponderance of the evidence* concept is a well-designed *reference list.* As with your letters of recommendation, the key here is to go "above and beyond" your competitors in providing real evidence of your capabilities.

As with the preceding example, most salespeople, when asked for references, will provide the names of two or three people. In the competitive sale, this is simply not good enough for the simple reason that your competitor will do the same thing—so we've really accomplished nothing in terms of value differentiation. Besides, is your prospective buyer supposed to be impressed that you have three happy customers? Think about it.

How Many Is Enough?

A reference list that meets the standard for total credibility will have— are you ready for this?—25 to 30 current customers. Before you shake your head at the task before you, be realistic: Doesn't your firm have 30 customers who would be willing, on request, to be an occasional reference for you? Of course you do! So this really isn't nearly the challenge that you think it is. All that you will need to do here is select them, call them, and ask them if they would be willing to participate. There is nothing more to it.

As you are putting this document together, you must ensure that you include for each of your references the following information:

1. *Contact information*—Meaning name, title, and company
2. *Street address, phone number, and e-mail address*
3. Most important—*a brief, two- to three-sentence description of what you are providing*

An example of a page from a reference list follows:

Springfield Times-Herald

Client References

CARITT JEWELERS
Lori Caritt, President
(704) 555–1212; lcarat@packjewelers.com

TMC program in place since January 2005. Run-of-site Internet advertising with downloadable discount coupon on purchases of $500 or more. Advertiser has experienced an increase of 11 percent in sales since initiating the advertising program.

PAY-MORE SHOES
Bob Loafer, General Manager
(321) 555–1234; ellis@pay-more.com

Pay-More has maintained a display ad in the Living Section of our newspaper on Friday mornings for the last three years. The company also regularly runs special sales promotions in the same section of the newspaper. Additionally, the company has run a quarterly insert in our publication for the last 12 months. Increase in gross sales of 28 percent since 2004.

BABY PLANET WORLD
Steve Toddler, Store Manager
(999) 555–1212; stoddler@BPW.com

Baby Planet World moved 80 percent of its advertising from radio to our reach products in June 2005 after disappointing results from that medium. We designed a comprehensive ad program that combined display ads, Internet banner ads containing a link to the BPW Web site, and a targeted direct-mail campaign to ZIP codes selected by family-based demographic data. Sales have improved by 22 percent since implementing this program.

FASHION MANSION
Daphne Mansion, President/Owner
(555)555–1212; MansionD@fashionmansion.com

Fashion Mansion is a boutique store that opened as a startup operation in January 2002. Since that time, this company has maintained a weekly presence in the Women's Day Section of our newspaper. In 2005, based on the success of this campaign, the same program was initiated online with a link to the company's Web site. Sales have grown at a double-digit rate for every year that the company has been an advertiser.

That last item—a description of what you provide the customer—is critical. When your buyer looks over your reference list, the first item he or she will look for is someone they know; the second, if available, is a situation similar to the one he or she is currently considering. By providing a brief description of each relationship, you actually motivate your prospect to check references by making it easy to find people who the prospective customer can relate to. Owing to the additional detail included, you are also producing a document that is seven to eight pages in length.

Once again, you will want to put a cover page on this stapled, finished document that says, "References from Satisfied Clients." As with the letters of recommendation, provide this document to your potential customer at the end of your first meeting. When you give this document to the prospective customer, say

"Here is a list of 30 clients with whom I work personally. I would like for you to call anyone you like and ask any questions that you have so that you can make a good business decision regarding our company."

This simple statement is powerful. It gives you total credibility with your prospective buyer. No competitors can approach your ability to demonstrate proven value. And when your prospect randomly calls your clients and hears consistently good reports, you will find invariably that you are the vendor of choice.

PREDATOR POINT

If you do not utilize proof of performance documentation, you have failed to eliminate risk—and you will usually lose the sale.

The Payoff: What's in It for You?

The collective effect of providing these three persuasion tools—biography sheets, letters of recommendation, and client references—is to lower the buyer's risk perception relative to your competition. Essentially, the message that you are communicating—overwhelmingly—is that your company does outstanding work. Your competitors simply will not address these critical issues in a way that approaches yours. Because you can provide a level of proof that is unmatched by other vendors, your buyer invariably will see you as the option with the least risk. Creating and using these "power tools" of persuasion will place you on a pedestal when competing for business—and will ensure that you become the front runner in virtually all your selling opportunities.

As a final point, you may have noticed that I ignored the issue of money throughout this chapter. Prepare yourself: This isn't going to change as you continue through this book. Assuming that your offerings are priced competitively, focusing on communicating value effectively is what wins sales. You are now armed with three weapons for winning more opportunities—biography sheets, letters of recommendation, and references. Next, we will look at how to prepare for the battles that await us on the competitive playing field.

Chapter | 2

DUE DILIGENCE

Establishing the Competitive Playing Field

Competitive sales are often won or lost before the first meeting actually takes place. Why? Because the seller who does his or her precall homework—and therefore knows more about the account going in than the competition—has a huge unfair advantage as the buying process is initiated. This chapter will show you how to get "locked and loaded" with data that your competitors simply overlook— and how to use this information to structure the initial meeting.

Most Competitive Sales Are RFPs

A basic yet critical characteristic of competitive selling opportunities is that they almost always begin as the result of an inquiry, or *request for proposal* (RFP). In other words, unlike prospected appointments, you are getting a call because the buyer has independently identified a need for what you provide and a decision already has been made to pursue it.

This fact of competitive sales is important because here the need to generate interest, a requirement of prospected or "cold" calls, is eliminated. Since the potential customer already recognizes a possible fit, you have much more latitude than you otherwise would when it comes to asking for information. We will review how to take full advantage of this situation shortly.

PREDATOR POINT

Always assume that an incoming inquiry is a competitive selling situation, until, or unless, you prove otherwise.

Most Initial Contacts Are Not Decision Makers

A second fact about incoming inquiries is that, in most cases, the person contacting you does not have any buying authority. Instead, this person is usually an information gatherer, or "influencer." This person has been assigned responsibility for collecting data and submitting it "upstairs" to the person or persons who actually make the buying decision.

This second point is neither good nor bad; it is simply how most businesses initiate buying decisions. Since this is a call-in lead, you must initially play the cards that you are dealt and work with your influencer. However, be aware that many of your competitors will, owing to a lack of strategy, continue to deal exclusively with this information gatherer during the entire competitive selling cycle. More on this later.

For now, recognize that, right out of the gate, you are dealing with two situational factors that can either assist or impede your ability to win competitive sales. Which direction these two factors take you depends largely on you. Think of the situation at this point as though you were being air dropped into unknown territory. As your parachute lowers you into the selling process, you need to immediately get your bearings and establish your perimeter.

Establishing Your Perimeter: The Seven-Question Interview

Because the potential customer has initiated an inquiry, your influencer has a built-in reason to cooperate with your need for information. While he or she rarely volunteers details, the initial contact almost always is cooperative when asked for details. In fact, the opening situation—that the potential customer, by contacting you, has demonstrated interest in a discussion—provides you with a gilded invitation to collect information for your initial meeting. This is a huge opportunity if it is handled properly. The key here, given that we have limited time on the phone, is to ask the right questions—in the right order—to learn as much as possible about the current state of the prospective buyer.

Most formal RFPs provide a contact person for questions. Whether responding to an RFP or handling an incoming phone call, the request should be as follows: "To make the best use of your time, do you have a moment to answer a few questions for me?" Because of the preestablished interest of the potential customer, the response you will get is, "Sure, what would you like to know?" Once you get this response, follow this seven-question sequence to lay the foundation for your strategy:

1. *How did you hear about us?* Predators always keep close tabs on where their leads are coming from. Enough said.

2. *What prompted you to contact us?* This will provide you with the *dominant buying motive*—the primary reason for the action taken in contacting you. Let the potential customer talk and take notes.

3. *What else can you tell me about what you are looking for?* This is often the most important question of the initial interview; this additional dig for more information can provide crucial details. In most cases it will provide you with secondary data about the desired outcomes of the prospective account— details that your competitors usually miss.

4. *What other options are you considering?* This is a subtle and nonthreatening way of asking, "Who is my competition?" Granted, the prospective account may refuse to share this with you—but this rarely happens. Worst case, the prospective account will not mind your asking. If you learn that competitors are being considered, immediately add the two "bonus" questions below:

   a. *Where are you in your meetings with them?* This establishes a pecking order. You usually will learn where you fall in the sequence of evaluating options, as well as how far along the account is in the decision process. If the prospective account already has met with your competition, add the following question:

   b. *What have you liked and not liked about what you've seen so far?* Again, the prospective account doesn't have to tell you this information—but what is the harm in asking? You might hit the jackpot. I once asked a prospect this question about one of my competitors, and his response was, "I disliked his presentation, and his pricing was out of line." Would you find this information useful? I did—and it helped me to easily land the account.

5. *What is your decision process, and who else besides you will be involved?* As we will discuss later, there is almost never a single person who buys without the input of others. It is critical that you identify this "inner circle" as quickly as possible. Don't be afraid to press for detail—"And what role does _____ have?"—and take notes!

6. *What is your role in this process?* This usually will clarify the level of influence that your initial contact has—or does not have—in the buying process. The most common response is, "My job is to gather information for them."

7. *What is your time frame for making a decision?* This is an excellent question to establish the interest level of the buyer and, incidentally, the quality of the lead. "We have to make a decision by _____" indicates a high-quality opportunity. "We are in no hurry" obviously indicates otherwise. "I'm not sure" translates to "I'm not high enough in our organization to know."

PREDATOR POINT

Callers will sometimes ask for a price over the phone. Respond by saying, "I will not be in a position to quote fees until after our initial meeting."

As the result of this brief fact-finding mission, you now know

- What marketing channel brought the prospect to you
- What the prospect's dominant buying motive is
- Secondary details regarding what the prospective account is looking for

- Who your competition is
- Where the prospect is in terms of his or her buying timeline, as well as your location as you enter the opportunity
- The prospect's initial assessment of your competitors
- The prospect's sense of urgency regarding the decision process

It is also worth noting here that as a result of asking these seven questions, you come across as being well organized, knowledgeable, and professional. Frankly, most people will be impressed with the way in which you conduct this interview. First impressions are important— and following this sequence allows you to put your best foot forward. Also, be aware that it is highly unlikely that your competition will ask for all this information. Because you did, you will begin the selling process armed with information that your competitors simply do not have. And by the time they get it—if they do at all—it is often too late.

A Note about E-mail

The preceding example assumes that the initial contact is made by a phone call. When responding to an e-mail inquiry, the best response method is always to respond via the telephone and personally introduce yourself. Unfortunately, some buyers do not initially want that up-close and personal experience. E-mail essentially allows them to talk to you without talking to you—and in some cases you will be forced to follow suit.

If you must communicate initially via e-mail, follow the same process outlined earlier for phone inquiries, but with a twist—formally submit your seven questions to the prospect as an attachment. Title this document "Client Premeeting Assessment," and leave space between each question for your prospect to encourage him or her to respond in detail. Ask the prospect to complete the form and send it back. Conclude your response by requesting a follow-up phone number so that you can discuss the prospect's responses with him or her after you have received the completed form.

An example of this e-mail document—and, for that matter, one that you can use as a guide when handling incoming phone calls—follows:

CLIENT PREMEETING ASSESSMENT

Please submit this completed form so that we may provide the information you requested. Thank you!

1. How did you hear about us?
2. What prompted you to contact us?
3. What can you tell me about what you are looking for?
4. What other options are you considering?

Now that we have armed ourselves with a framework in which to operate, we are ready for our initial meeting with the person who contacted us. The remainder of this chapter will outline how to handle this first encounter.

The Three Influencer Traps

As noted earlier, the person who contacts you in the competitive sale usually does not have buying authority; he or she frequently is gathering information on someone else's behalf. The standard operational procedure (SOP) being employed here by your influencer is to meet with you, see what you have, and then forward your information to the people who actually requested it. This is illustrated in Figure 2.1, with S being you, the salesperson, I being your initial contact, or influencer, and the others being the people to whom your influencer plans to present your information.

Figure 2.1

The Selling "Wall".

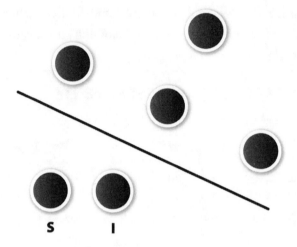

S I

Chapter 2 will discuss in detail how to get over this "selling wall" and interact with the others in the buying process. First, however, it is important to discuss what *not* to do here—by avoiding three traps that your competitors are likely to fall into during the initial meeting phase.

Influencer Trap 1: The Window Shopper

The one fundamental liability that the influencer poses to your success in the competitive sale is his or her lack of authority to choose among options. Simply stated, this is a person who can say "No" but not "Yes" to any of you. In other words, if your influencer isn't on board with your recommendations, he or she has the power to eliminate you from the pool of consideration. However, if he or she is completely enamored of what you offer, it doesn't really matter because he or she can't make the vendor selection. Therefore, the best possible outcome that you have with the influencer is that he or she doesn't say "No." You cannot win competitive sales by having people not say no; you will need at some point to talk to the person or people with the power to say "Yes."

Despite this, most of your competitors will make the fundamental mistake of presenting pricing to the influencer when inevitably asked to do so. This is the first of three *influencer traps* because once your influencer has your competitor's fees or pricing, he or she has no further need for your competitor's involvement in the decision process. Vendors who fall into this trap simply shut the door on their chances for winning.

PREDATOR POINT

Never present pricing exclusively to a person who cannot buy what you are selling. Let your competitors do that.

Influencer Trap 2: The Delusional Deputy

To complicate matters further, it is not uncommon for your influencer to be under the delusion that he or she has buying authority when, in fact, he or she has nothing of the kind. If you have been in sales for any length of time, you surely have witnessed this affliction.

I certainly have, including this memorable episode: Some years ago I was contacted by the executive vice president of an insurance company for a rather large opportunity regarding my firm's services. Because of this person's title, I made the assumption (my first mistake, of course—you should *never* assume) that he had the authority to make a decision. We had a productive first meeting, and I was asked to submit a proposal, which I promptly did. He informed me that I would be hearing back with a faxed letter of agreement if we were to be working together.

Several days later—it was, as I recall, a beautiful Friday afternoon in the spring, and the birds were chirping and the sun was shining— our fax machine lit up, and I was delighted to see, as expected, that the incoming pages had this insurance company's logo prominently displayed at the top of the first page. Yes, this was the anticipated letter from the executive informing me that we were moving forward.

To celebrate this new opportunity, I loaded up the staff for a trip to our local watering hole (it was a Friday afternoon, after all), and I spent a significant sum of company "petty cash" on various alcoholic libations and bar-food goodies well into the evening. After all, we had a done deal and had reason to celebrate, right?

Then Monday morning arrived. Monday was a cold, cloudy day, and the birds weren't chirping and the sun wasn't shining, and at approximately 10 a.m. my fax machine lit up again. This fax had the same logo as the one received on Friday afternoon, but the message was starkly different: Essentially it said, "We regret to inform you that the proposal heretofore approved has since been deapproved. Thank you for your time."

What happened? Nothing more complicated than my executive vice president taking my proposal to the CEO—a person who happened to have final approval authority—and promptly being shot out of the saddle. So much for Friday afternoon "happy hour."

The lesson here? Don't fall into the trap of assuming that your "decision maker" knows what he or she is talking about. If you have doubts about your influencer's claim to be the buyer, ask this question: "What person or group will be most affected by the decision that you will be making?" This person, or the head of this group, then becomes the top priority on your must-contact list. More about this later.

Influencer Trap 3: The Apathetic Acolyte

Finally, in the scenario described, your influencer almost never has a personal stake in the decision outcome. Once he or she gathers data and submits information from all competitors "upstairs," he or she is rarely affected personally by the selection being made. The point is, if you aren't getting access to people with a stake in the outcome, you aren't able to differentiate your value proposition from your competition; this person simply doesn't have a reason to care.

A classic example of this dilemma is the role of the purchasing agent. Legions of salespeople sell exclusively to purchasing, wrongly assuming that this is their decision maker. Then they wonder why virtually every decision they get from this group is based exclusively on the lowest price, correspondingly devoid of profit and reduced to a simple commodity selection without regard to value.

Purchasing agents, in many cases, are not true decision makers. Most commonly they make acquisitions based on the needs and directives of others in the company. Put another way, when someone needs something, he or she calls purchasing to requisition that item for the department in need. Purchasing's primary—and in some cases, their only—role is to negotiate the lowest possible cost for the item. This is an important and necessary function within any business—but also one that has nothing to do with the issue of value. In fact, the argument can be made that nobody in the company has less of a personal stake in what you are selling than the purchasing department. After all, once the item is delivered, how well it performs is not purchasing's concern—that issue becomes the domain of the end user. If you want to sell value, let your competitors slave away in the salt mines of purchasing. You should be doing your business elsewhere.

A Note about Online Bidding

Most of us have come to realize, through trial and error, that not all advancements in technology turn out to be a step in the right direction. Case in point: Purchasing managers of some companies have begun using a procedure known as *online bidding* to order products and services from suppliers.

This new way of conducting business is modeled after the online auction company eBay and works as follows: When a need arises within a company for goods or services, purchasing sends out an e-mail to multiple suppliers requesting bids for the opportunity. Salespeople who wish to participate then submit "quotes" to the e-mail address of the company requesting the bid. In this new selling environment, there are no meetings, no discussions of needs, no relationships, and no loyalty. You simply submit a price and wait for a reply. If your bid is not as low as a competitor, you receive a boilerplate e-mail that says, in effect, "Sorry, you did not submit the lowest bid; however, feel free to grovel further."

Surely some bright, well-meaning individual came up with this concept, and it seems to be catching on like wildfire with those minions whose measurement of success is getting a pat on the head for shaving a nickel here and a dime there. There is but one appropriate method for responding to an online bid request: In as polite and professional a manner as possible, treat these incoming e-mails like the "spam" they are, and inform those who send them your way that (1) your company is not in business to be the least expensive option, (2) your time is valuable, and (3) you and your company are not commodities. In other words, tell them to take a flying leap.

Why? Because doing business with these companies is a dead-end road. Any potential account with no more regard for what you provide than to waste your time in this manner is not a company with which you want to do business. Companies that want to play a game of penny-ante with you should be excluded from your customer base.

Why Not Just Go Over the Influencer's Head?

Given these influencer-driven obstacles, it is natural for salespeople to want to go around their influencer and climb the chain of command. Many sales training programs that I have attended implore salespeople to "go to the top" and "sell directly to the decision maker." This sounds great in theory, right? Unfortunately, in competitive selling situations, it is neither practical nor productive—not at first.

The reason is simple and straightforward: As noted earlier, this is an incoming lead. As such, the person who contacted you, like it or not, has been appointed to serve in an official capacity on behalf of the others in the buying decision. Leapfrogging this person therefore isn't a viable option—but then, fortunately, it does not need to be.

From a practical standpoint, your influencer has several attributes that make it in your best interest to work with him or her collaboratively:

- He or she is an excellent source of information—in some cases, the best source—regarding the basic needs of the prospect.
- He or she can become a strong ally of yours if you treat him or her with the courtesy and respect due his or her position.
- As a "gatekeeper," he or she can provide you or, if he or she chooses, deny you access to the others in the buying decision. (I will discuss how to get this access later in the book.)

The Initial Meeting: What Is Your Objective?

In my years of work as a sales consultant, I rode in the field with dozens of salespeople on sales calls. When we got in the car, the first question that I would routinely ask as we embarked on an appointment was this: "What is our objective for this initial sales call?"

In order, the most common responses I would get to this question were

- To identify the needs of the prospective account
- To establish rapport with the initial contact
- To identify the decision maker(s)
- To make an effective presentation

In your opinion, which of these four choices is the objective for the initial meeting? Or would none of these fit your definition of this objective?

If you answered, "None of the above," you are correct! All these are steps in a process—and none of them therefore qualifies as an objective. Let me explain.

Your objective in an initial meeting is found in the answer to this question: "If this meeting goes as planned, what is the desired next step—in other words, what is our destination?" When you frame the issue in these terms, there is only one logical answer: *a second meeting to include the others in the decision process.* Period. Thus, in most cases, your objective in a first meeting is a second meeting with those who will be involved in the decision process.

The implications of coming into the competitive buying process with an objective established and a plan for accomplishing that objective cannot be stressed enough in the competitive sale. As buyers evaluate you and your competitors, one option among you will quickly emerge as the front-runner in every competitive selling opportunity: The competitor who is best prepared—meaning the one who knows where he or she is going and has a practical strategy for getting there— naturally will assume this leadership position. This pecking order is established both with the buyer(s) and relative to competition.

Now that we know our objective for this first meeting, let's examine our strategy for accomplishing this objective.

The Structure of the Initial Consultation

To secure a second meeting with the "inner circle," the initial consultation meeting is composed of the following six steps in this order:

1. Establish rapport with the initial contact.
2. Use an agenda to establish control of the meeting.
3. Conduct an initial needs analysis to identify baseline needs.
4. Deliver a conceptual presentation to establish your viability as a solution provider.
5. Identify the "inner circle."
6. Close for the second meeting.

The remainder of this chapter will focus on establishing rapport and using an agenda to establish control of the meeting.

Establishing Rapport in the Competitive Sale

You already know the importance of establishing rapport with new buyers. You also know that buying influencers share information with people with whom they feel comfortable; otherwise, this meeting is likely to be a waste of time.

There is no question that being "liked" by your initial contact is important. Establishing rapport early gives you another competitive advantage as we begin the discovery process. However, there is more to establishing rapport than simply being "liked." There is also a right way—and a very wrong way—to do this. Let's begin by looking at how *not* to establish rapport.

When I began my sales career, my first training program taught me to establish rapport in this way: Look around the person's office and desk, find something that you can use as a conversation starter, and comment on it. Sound familiar? It certainly was to a sales rep I rode with a few years ago because I witnessed this conversation between him and a CFO/buyer:

Salesperson *(points to picture):* "Your daughter is very attractive."
CFO *(stares blankly at salesperson):* "Actually, that's my wife."

Faux pas aside, there is another negative implication of the old "find something in common" approach to rapport building: You are wasting the person's time. After all, the person called you in because he or she has a business need to discuss; when you begin a conversation on an unrelated topic, you are likely to cause the prospect to quickly become bored and impatient. (If you want to talk about golf or fishing, do so at the end of the meeting, not at the beginning.)

Is there a better way? Fortunately, yes. In his timeless book, *How to Win Friends and Influence People*, Dale Carnegie points out that the two things that people like to talk about the most are *themselves* and *their business*. In our day and time, an almost foolproof way to leverage this simple concept is to begin with a question about the business based on information available to you from precall preparation.

To establish good rapport, every time, with buyers in competitive sales, follow these steps:

1. Go to the company's Web site, and print it at your office. Staple the document, and place it in your folder for the account.
2. Read the Web site information in your car, and pull several items for discussion from what you learn.
3. Arrive 10 minutes early for your scheduled appointment.
4. Use one of the items as a conversation starter with your initial contact to open the meeting.

Examples:

"Janice, in looking over your company's Web site, I read that your company is planning to _____. What can you tell me about that?"

"Mike, your Web site states that your firm is now operating in 12 states. What are your growth plans for the next three to five years?"

This line of questioning not only gives you a great way to open a discussion, but it also shows the prospect that you had enough interest in his or her business to research the company before the meeting—which by itself serves to place you in a favorable light with the initial contact.

You actually accomplish two objectives with this rapport-building strategy: First, you demonstrate that you prepared for the meeting by researching the company, and second, you get your new contact to open up to you by referencing a talking point of interest to him or her and the company. Rapport building accomplished, we now move to the agenda.

How to Use an Agenda to Establish Control

An overriding theme that flows continuously throughout the competitive selling cycle (and throughout this book) is the concept of *sales leadership*. Predators do not "push" buyers; they *lead* them. They come to the competitive sale with a well-designed methodology, and buyers follow them because predators make it clear that they have the confidence and expertise to help their customers make a well-informed business decision. Predators demonstrate through their behavior and know-how that their recommendations are the most logical choice for the potential customer. Nowhere in the sales process is this concept of leadership more evident than with the use of an agenda to begin the initial consultation.

It is important to remember that to separate yourself from competitive options, you must establish an environment in which the prospect will provide you with a candid and detailed description of his or her company's current issues so that you have the foundation necessary to recommend solutions. To review: In order for this meeting to be mutually productive, you will need to conduct—with the complete cooperation of your influencer—an analysis of needs. You will need time to present and discuss potential solutions to those needs. You then will want to identify the decision process and, finally, wrap up the discussion by gaining agreement from the influencer to have a second meeting with the others in that process.

Once rapport has been established, the time comes to set this process in motion by introducing an agenda for the meeting.

The Structure of the Agenda

An effective agenda for sales calls will have three parts:

The opening. The opening of the agenda serves to shift the
discussion from rapport building to the business at hand. It
should be a consultative, leading statement such as
"Here is what I would like to do today"

The procedure. The procedure outlines the steps the discussion
will follow, in order. Usually, an initial meeting consultation
will be presented in the following three steps:
"First, I would like to ask you a few questions about your
current situation and about your business to better understand
what you are looking for."
"Then I will give you a brief overview of our capabilities based
on the information you provide."
"Finally, if there is mutual interest at the end of this meeting,
we can discuss options for a next step."

The close. The close simply asks for agreement to follow the plan
you just presented. To close for agreement, simply say, "Would
this be acceptable to you?"

If you follow this concept in presenting your agenda, you will find,
virtually 100 percent of the time, that the response you get to the question, "Would this be acceptable to you?" is "Yes, that's fine." It is
important to note what implications the word *yes* has here. By agreeing to your agenda, your influencer has just given you complete control of the meeting. You now have his or her permission to run the
show—in other words, to conduct your needs analysis, review your
capabilities, and close for the second meeting. How do you feel at this
point about the likelihood of your accomplishing this key objective?

Also, let's revisit that *sales leadership* issue again here. Think for a moment about the impression that your influencer will have of you at this early point in the competitive selling process. If I were to ask the influencer, "What is your initial impression of this person?" I would receive feedback as follows:

- Confident
- Knowledgeable
- Interested in my opinion and my needs
- Well organized
- Professional
- Not going to waste my time
- Not going to push something on me

When you consider the fact that your initial contact is evaluating other competitors, this first impression has significant implications. You are, in effect, setting a high bar for your competitors to meet. In my experience, most of them will not follow a well-defined process such as the one I have just presented. Instead, they will "wing it." They will lack a cohesive strategy, and you will establish yourself as the front-runner in the first 10 minutes of your initial meeting.

So let's review what has just taken place:

- You have established good rapport with your influencer.
- You have established that you are well organized, professional, and not going to waste his or her time.
- You have been given permission by the influencer to run the meeting.
- Your influencer has agreed to discuss a next step if he or she is interested.

Now that you have been given permission to lead the meeting, the next step, per our agenda, becomes asking a few questions about the company's current situation. The most important skill in the process—and, incidentally, the one that affects your success in winning competitive opportunities most directly—is the *client needs analysis.* I will outline how to structure and execute this step in Chapter 3.

Chapter | 3

THE NOTORIOUS D.I.G.

How to Conduct the Client Needs Analysis

Early in my sales career I developed the habit of listening to audio training programs while driving to sales calls in my car. Of all the sales and motivational experts I listened to in those years, my favorite was the great sales trainer and speaker Brian Tracy. His audio program, "The Psychology of Success," remains my all-time favorite to this day.

Of the many excellent points that he shared regarding selling to decision makers, one that made a particularly strong impact was this: "I would much rather talk about what I need than hear about what you have."

This may well be the best single sentence of sales advice that I ever received.

You already know the importance of asking good questions. All salespeople do, but many lack a good structure for executing this key skill. This chapter will teach you how to use a *client needs analysis* to interview prospective clients and, most important, to identify needs that your competitors overlook.

Public versus Private Information

Invariably, when buyers evaluate multiple vendors, the vendor whose recommendations most closely match the buyer's needs will win the business. This sounds simple enough. The problem—and the opportunity—presented to you lies in the fact that need-based information volunteered by your prospect also will be made available to your competitors. In competitive selling, we refer to this as *public information*. These are the primary needs that the client has already identified and ones that will be shared freely with you and your competitors.

If you are building a proposal strictly from public information—in other words, from the same stated objectives that your competitors work from—it is a foregone conclusion that your proposal will look the same as theirs does. This is not the way to differentiate your value proposition.

Of significantly more importance and value to Predators is *private information*. This is the information that your competitors never ask for and therefore overlook. Private information exists as unstated needs because either (1) the prospect has not yet realized that these issues are present or (2) other people in the company have these issues, but they were not communicated to the initial contact with whom you are working during the initial phase of the buying process.

If you want to distinguish yourself from other potential vendors and win the account, you must know how to obtain *secondary information*. You must become a *notorious D.I.G.*—a "notoriously detailed information gatherer."

Proactive versus Reactive Interviewing

Most of your competitors will conduct a *reactive* interview with the influencer. This means that they will use the information provided in the initial inquiry as their sole basis for asking questions. For example, if the influencer's stated purchase objectives are to improve product quality, customer satisfaction, and operating efficiency, your competitors' questions will revolve exclusively around these three topics — product quality, customer satisfaction, and operating efficiency. The only attempt at finding secondary needs will occur at the end of the meeting, and it usually will be a single question: "Is there anything else that we haven't discussed?"

This is where notorious D.I.G.s set the stage for winning the business. Yes, the notorious D.I.G. also investigates the primary information topics, but they will then move to a completely different, secondary interview strategy that gathers private information — data not volunteered or shared with competitors. The most important skill in this environment — and, incidentally, the most difficult to master — is becoming adept at ferreting out private information via an effective client needs analysis. How to go about structuring and executing this most critical selling step is what I will cover next.

PREDATOR POINT

Private Information is the key to separating your value proposition from your competitors, and winning the sale.

Needles in a Haystack

To understand the importance of private information to your selling success, visualize the potential customer's account as a haystack. There are needles throughout this haystack: visible ones, which represent public information, and buried ones, which represent private information. You and your competitors have unfettered access to the visible needles, which all of you will collect from the hay. In terms of value, think of the visible needles as being made of silver and the hidden ones as being made of gold.

Because your competitors will focus exclusively on collecting visible needles, their proposals will all look the same. Your information base will not rely exclusively on public information, so your recommendations will provide considerably more value to the prospect. However, you need a methodology to find the more valuable golden needles.

There are two ways to accomplish this. The first, which is virtually useless, is to throw handfuls of hay into the air until, perhaps, a golden needle falls out. The selling equivalent of this method is what a lot of salespeople do, which is essentially to tell the potential customer about everything that you offer and hope that you trip over something of interest to them.

A much more effective methodology is to use the communications equivalent of a metal detector—by first knowing where you expect to find the golden needles and then by going directly to where you expect them to be.

Private Information Topics (PITs)

The first step in this process is to temporarily set aside what you know from the public information provided and think like your potential customer does. As a notorious D.I.G. who sells to this type of account, you already know from experience where the golden needles in the haystack are most likely to exist—in other words, where problems or shortcomings are likely to be in the ways in which this company conducts its business. These areas will be the basis for your secondary interview and will be treated as individual discussion topics during the first meeting. I will refer to these as *private information topics* (PITs) because they were not communicated to the vendor list at the time of the request for proposals (RFP).

PREDATOR POINT

You should have between five and seven Private Information Topics (PITs) prepared for the first meeting.

Predator PITs: Two Examples

How does this thought process actually work in a selling opportunity? Here are two simple examples from diverse industries in which I have previous experience as a consultant/trainer.

Example 1

Type of business of buyer: Casual-dining restaurant chain with 22 locations

Seller: Distributor of restaurant equipment

Public information provided to all potential vendors: The restaurant chain has stated in the RFP that it wishes to purchase a two-well, large-capacity fryer for each location that is capable of handling 100 pounds of fried foods (french fries, wings, etc.) on a daily basis. The chain has provided product specifications regarding capacity, unit size, and temperature requirements.

PITs for the interview:

- *Labor costs.* Investigate the importance of ease of use and cleaning times in the unit purchase relative to available kitchen staff labor.
- *Menu plans.* Learn of the chain's future plans to expand or change the existing menu, especially with regard to fried foods.

- *Foot traffic.* Investigate the chain's satisfaction level with the number of patrons it is currently attracting to its restaurant locations.
- *Average check.* Determine the chain's approximate average per-visit check and its interest level in increasing this figure.
- *Market differentiation.* Learn what the chain does to distinguish itself from its competitors, and determine its need to enhance this.
- *Customer profile.* Establish the ideal customer for the chain, and look for ways to attract more of these potential customers to the stores.

In this example, we can expect the other vendors to focus exclusively on selling a fryer. The notorious D.I.G. knows that the key to winning the account is to focus on finding and providing solutions to business problems that may or may not involve the needs stated solely for frying equipment.

Example 2

Type of business of buyer: Real estate brokerage

Seller: Newspaper advertising account executive

Public information provided to all potential vendors: The real estate brokerage has announced that it plans to invest in an advertising campaign to build visibility in the local market. The company is requesting proposals from various media for attaining this increased market awareness.

PITs for the interview:

- *Current situation.* What does the firm currently do to advertise, and what is its satisfaction level with the medium that it is currently using?

- *Demographics.* What is the average sales price of the homes that the brokerage markets? What are the demographics of the people who purchase them? How important is it to the brokerage firm to focus its market awareness objectives on this audience?
- *Qualified buyers.* Given the higher, stricter standards of lenders, what has the brokerage firm's experience been in attracting financially qualified home buyers? How important is it to the brokerage firm to ensure that financially qualified buyers are the recipients of its marketing message?
- *Listings.* What has been the brokerage's success rate in attracting listings from sellers? Is there a need to attract listings as a part of the advertising campaign?
- *Inventory.* How large an inventory of unsold homes is the brokerage currently carrying? Besides market awareness, is an objective of the advertising campaign to clear unsold inventory?

In this second situation, we can expect the other media outlets to prepare a proposal that addresses one concern: the public information–based issue of increasing visibility in the community. The notorious D.I.G. is prepared to also make advertising recommendations for targeting demographics, attracting qualified buyers, increasing listings, and moving unsold inventory—depending, of course, on how these issues are affecting the brokerage business objectives.

You can readily see the implications of this approach in the competitive sale. One of the proposals submitted in this process will offer significantly more value than the others because the Predator involved in each case built a solution based on both public *and* private information.

Predator PITs: An Exercise

Now that you understand the logic behind PITs, take a few minutes to create, on the worksheet below, your own list of areas that you will want to investigate with future competitive selling opportunities. Select a business type or industry to which you sell to frequently, and identify five potential areas of need that you know from experience that this type of potential customer is likely to have. These obviously also need to be areas where you can provide value in terms of either (1) a solution to a problem or (2) the ability to improve or expand an already good situation.

PITs Worksheet

Type of Business/Industry: _____

Potential PITS:

1. _____

   How can this situation potentially affect the account's business?

2. _____

   How can this situation potentially affect the account's business?

3. _____

   How can this situation potentially affect the account's business?

4. _____

   How can this situation potentially affect the account's business?

5. _____

   How can this situation potentially affect the account's business?

Now look over the list you've created, and ask yourself this question: How many businesses in the industry you selected are completely happy with every one of the topics that you just listed?

Isn't the answer basically "Zero"?

This should be a powerful revelation to you because in essence it proves that virtually every single account that you call on has a need for what you provide. Therefore, when initial meetings don't go well, the problem is not that the prospect has no needs but rather that most salespeople don't know how to find those needs.

PREDATOR POINT

If you develop your PITs properly, virtually every account that you encounter will have a need, or needs, for what you offer.

Why is this so often the case?

The Four Steps of Developing Needs

You have probably heard the old adage that good salespeople are good listeners. This really isn't an accurate statement. You are probably also familiar with the idea that a salesperson should do about 20 percent of the talking in an interview, with the buyer doing the remaining 80 percent. This is true, but it doesn't normally just happen by itself in a meeting. Allow me to explain.

Notorious D.I.G.s really aren't good listeners; they are good *askers of questions*. In other words, the skill employed is not listening nearly as much as knowing how to interview properly. If you ask the right *sequence of questions*, the result is that the buyer does most of the talking.

Despite this, many salespeople don't structure questions properly. They don't understand the difference between a needs interview and a survey. Such questions as "Are you happy with ____? and "Is _____ working well for you?" are survey questions—they are answered with a "Yes" or a "No." They uncover nothing. They provide little, if any, useful information. Further, they bore the person you are interviewing.

Your goal in the meeting is to have a meaningful dialogue in which your influencer freely shares information that is relevant to his or her employer's needs and to your later recommendations. To accomplish this, you introduce your PITs to the influencer with the use of *topic-opening questions*.

Topic-Opening Questions

You already know the value of using open-ended questions, which are those that cannot be answered with a "Yes" or a "No." Topic-opening questions are similar, except that they are specialized: They open your PITs for discussion with your influencer.

Let's return to the sales call we left in Chapter 2. We have opened the meeting by introducing ourselves. We have established rapport by referencing a printout of the company's Web site and asking the influencer to comment on it. We have used an agenda ("Here is what I would like to do today") to establish control of the meeting. We have been given permission to proceed.

Because we were called into this opportunity, the prospect will want to first address whatever issues or needs prompted him or her to contact you and your competitors. With this in mind, we begin the interview with these previously known public information topic(s). The first question we always ask in the competitive sale is "What are you looking for?" "Could you begin by telling me more about what you are trying to accomplish?"

Your influencer will respond by explaining the company's public information needs; keep in mind that this information will be shared, almost verbatim, with your competition. Let the influencer speak, uninterrupted. Then ask any additional questions that you deem appropriate until you completely understand what issue(s) prompted the prospect to initiate the buying process.

Now we transition to the important part of the interview.

The Secondary Needs Analysis

Using your PITs list, select a single topic, or "needle," for discussion, and then ask a broad, topic-opening question that prompts your influencer to begin talking about the subject. Good topic-opening questions, like open-ended questions, require a detailed answer. Examples:

"Give me an overview of . . ."

"What has been your experience with . . ."

"What is your satisfaction level with . . ."

The purpose of each topic-opening question is to introduce, one at a time, your PITs to the influencer to determine whether or not a situation exists that may offer opportunities for you. Each topic-opening question that you ask should be a broad-based attempt to open a dialog on *one particular aspect* of the prospect's needs. Each of these areas should be investigated separately, with resolution achieved on whether or not a selling opportunity exists prior to moving on to another topic.

To illustrate, let's refer to one of the examples cited earlier in this chapter: the advertising sales rep with a real estate brokerage firm that wants to advertise. Our notorious D.I.G. knows from the RFP that the firm wants to use advertising to increase visibility in the community. This is public information. The ad rep begins the interview by discussing the public information item first. He or she says to the influencer, "Tell me more about what you want to accomplish in terms of visibility." The influencer provides this information, just as he or she will to the competition.

Now the ad rep switches gears. For purposes of gathering private information, the ad rep has identified five PITs that he or she wants to review with the influencer. In the example provided earlier, these were

- Satisfaction with current advertising efforts
- Reaching targeted demographics
- Finding qualified home buyers
- Securing listings from home sellers
- Moving the existing inventory of homes

The ad rep then selects one of the five PITs just listed to begin the private information, or secondary, interview. In this case, the ad rep decides to begin with the topic of securing listings. An appropriate topic-opening question is, "What has your experience been this year with regard to obtaining listings from home sellers?"

Reading the Response

If you structure your questions properly when opening each topic, you will immediately learn in each case whether or not a potential need exists. Specifically, you will get one of two basic responses to each PIT question you ask, as shown in Figure 3.1: either (1) "We are very happy with that"—which indicates that no opportunity exists—or (2) something else, indicating that an opportunity does exist.

"Something else" rarely manifests as, "Funny that you ask; I'm having a big problem with that." This would be too easy. In practice, if a need exists, by far the most common response you will get is a neutral statement such as

"Overall, it's not bad."

"We are holding steady."

Figure 3.1

The two basic responses to PITs questions.

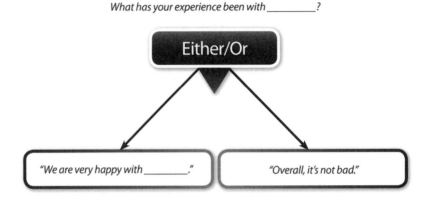

What has your experience been with _____?

Either/Or

"We are very happy with _____."   *"Overall, it's not bad."*

"Given the economy, we are doing pretty well."

This is how most buyers reveal potential needs, and it is also the point at which most salespeople stumble.

Most salespeople know what to do with the statement, "We are very happy with _____." Since there isn't a problem with this aspect of the business, the appropriate thing to do is to drop the subject and move on to another topic. However, most don't know what to do with a response such as "Overall, it's not bad." They assume that such mundane statements also indicate no selling opportunity—when, in fact, they do just the opposite.

You need to be different. You need to recognize the opportunity being presented here—and you need to know how to develop it.

PREDATOR POINT

Buyers almost never reveal existing needs in graphic terms. Instead, they will use conservative, neutral ways to describe existing problems.

Directive Questioning

In our example, the real estate broker's response to the question about the number of listings being generated was "Overall, it's not bad." Our notorious D.I.G. sees that this represents a potential opportunity. He or she develops it by asking a *directive question*—one that further directs, or develops, the initial statement made by the influencer.

Directive questions are structured as follows:

"When you say _____, what do you mean by that?"

Thus, in our example, our notorious D.I.G.'s question becomes

"When you say 'Overall, it's not bad,' what do you mean by that?"

Notice here that the ad rep has restated the influencer's initial comment and asked him or her to elaborate on it. If you think about it, you can readily see what is going to happen next. This question will have the influencer, in effect, present the existing problem directly to the salesperson:

"What I mean by 'It's not bad' is _____."

Typically, the response will sound something like:

"What I mean by 'It's not bad' is that we are down in listings by about 20 percent from this time last year, but given the state of the economy, that is to be expected."

Consider the situation at this point: The ad rep introduced the topic of listings. Using an appropriate topic-opening question, he or she identified a potential issue regarding the number of listings being generated. Next, by using a directive question to explore further, the ad rep has confirmed that an opportunity exists.

Consequence Questioning

What the ad rep does not know at this point—and what will determine the extent of the influencer's interest in a solution—is how the existing situation of declining listings is affecting the brokerage's business. In other words, we know so far that listings are down 20 percent from the previous year. We do not know what impact this situation is having on the health of the company. This is what really matters—and this needs to be determined by the salesperson.

Consequence questions, as the name implies, are used to do this—to determine how an existing situation is affecting the influencer's business. Consequence questions are structured as follows:

"How is [the current situation] affecting [business]?"

Our notorious D.I.G. therefore asks the Influencer:

"How is the fact that your listings are down 20 percent from last year affecting the company's ability to meet agent sales goals?"

To which the Influencer likely replies:

"It's having a significant negative impact on our bottom line."

Now we are getting somewhere. Our notorious D.I.G. knows that the issue of obtaining listings is an important one to the client. It is an area that is causing a significant problem for the company. The only thing left to do now is to confirm the obvious—to gain agreement that the prospect would be interested in doing something about it.

Confirming Questions

Confirming questions are used to wrap up the topic being discussed by verifying that the influencer is interested in a solution to the stated problem. The structure of confirming questions is as follows:

"If we could _____ so that _____, would you be open to _____?"

Therefore, with regard to the issue of listings, our notorious D.I.G. asks our influencer:

"If we could provide you with a way to increase the number of listings generated so that you could improve the sales performance of your agents, would you be open to taking a look at what we can do for you in this area?"

This is a dumb question; the only logical answer is "Of course we would." Despite this, it needs to be asked; we need our influencer to verbally confirm his or her interest. The ad rep now has developed a secondary need opportunity, overlooked by the competition, that will be included in the proposal to come later.

To review: We use a four-step question process for the secondary needs analysis:

- *Topic opening*—"What has your experience been with _____?"
- *Directing*—"What do you mean by _____?"
- *Consequence*—"How is _____ affecting your business?"
- *Confirming*—"If we could ____ so that _____, would you be open to ____?"

This simple four-step process is the key to developing secondary (unstated) needs. Interview meetings with potential buyers therefore are a series of five to seven miniature interviews on various PITs presented, one at a time, by the salesperson. By presenting our PITs for discussion, directing the discussion, establishing consequences, and confirming buy-in, we have the power to create opportunities for value-based selling where none were identified previously. This skill, more than any other factor, will determine our success in winning competitive selling opportunities.

A Word of Caution

As we conclude our review of the needs analysis, it is important that you know how to handle situations where influencer interest threatens to derail the interview. When we confirm with the influencer that he or she would be open to taking a look at a solution to a problem, a common reaction that you will get is, "Sure I would—what do you have?" This means that he or she wants to know—immediately—what your solution looks like. Do you answer the question, or do you postpone your answer until later in the meeting?

The request by the influencer is appropriate and completely understandable. Unfortunately, the worst possible thing that you can do is immediately agree to this request—and give in to the urge to start selling.

Why? Because once you start explaining benefits, the interview is over! Let's not forget about all the other PITs that we had planned on investigating. If you fall into the trap of discussing solutions prematurely, those other discussion topics fall by the wayside. This happens the moment that you shift from asking questions to offering solutions. It also causes you to lose control of the agenda and of the interview process.

Therefore, the only appropriate way to handle this request is to politely put it off by saying, "If you will just bear with me for a few minutes, I will go over what we offer in detail at the end of our meeting. In the meantime, however, there are a few other areas of your business that I would like to discuss first. Would this be okay with you?" The response you will get is, "Yes, that's fine." Now that you have regained control of the conversation, you can move on to your next "needle."

PREDATOR POINT

Refrain from sharing your ability to provide solutions until you have completed the Needs Analysis.

The remainder of the meeting then becomes a series of "mini-interviews" whereby you introduce your PITs, one at a time, and determine in each case whether or not that topic presents a problem for the influencer and an opportunity for you. As noted earlier, in a typical first meeting, you should plan on presenting five to seven individual PITs for discussion with your influencer. Of these five to seven topics, you can expect, on average, to have two of them produce opportunities; in all other cases, the response you will get will be, essentially, "We are happy with that."

When this happens, it is not a setback. It is simply the current state of the prospective account. In fact, you can win competitive sales with just one "golden needle." Find two of them, and winning the account becomes a virtual lock. Finding three or more is an exceptionally rare event. All other topics will have a common denominator: "That's not a problem for us."

This concludes the interview process. Once you have, through this questioning sequence, arrived at this point, you will have a clear understanding of

- What the secondary, private information issues are in the company
- How each of these issues is affecting the business
- The interest level of the influencer in addressing each issue

None of your competitors will have any of this information, and none of them will address these issues in their proposals. Now you are armed with the information you need to clearly stand out from your competition and win the business.

However, it is not time to get up and leave the meeting.

Recall that in our agenda from Chapter 2 we stated that we would give the influencer "a brief overview of our capabilities." Your influencer has just answered your questions. During the interview, you told him or her that you had potential solutions to issues that you uncover. He or she naturally wants to know what these are. Now that the interview is concluded, it is time to present those capabilities.

Concluding the Needs Analysis: The Conceptual Presentation

The *conceptual presentation* is an informal overview that provides your influencer with a description of your capabilities based on his or her answers to your questions. It addresses his or her immediate need for information and verifies that you have a good fit between private information needs and your offerings. However, it does not represent your final recommendations, and it does not include pricing. Think of the conceptual presentation as an informal discussion, a review of ways in which your firm may—the key operative word here being *may*—be of value to the prospective account.

The Suite-of-Solutions Wheel

You have probably heard the saying "A picture is worth a thousand words." A fundamental error that most salespeople make at this point is a failure to provide supporting visual tools to reinforce the value propositions made in the initial meeting. In other words, they ignore the power of "show and tell"—the fact that most people remember information much better if they see and hear it as opposed to simply hearing it.

A simple yet highly effective visual aid that will profoundly improve your ability to deliver an effective conceptual presentation is called the *suite-of-solutions wheel*. This single-page concept is a visual diagram that provides the salesperson with "talking points" for a discussion of solution capabilities. An example of this is presented in Figure 3.2.

Your company name occupies the center, or hub, of the diagram. The spokes that emanate out from the center each represent core product or service solutions that your company provides the marketplace.

Figure 3.2

A suite-of-solutions wheel.

Using the Suite-of-Solutions Wheel in the Meeting

At the conclusion of your needs analysis, thank your influencer for answering your questions. At this point, bring out your suite-of-solutions wheel and say, "As you can see by this diagram, our company offers a complete range of services and solutions for our clients' needs. At this point, I would like to review the issues that you shared with me earlier, and I will describe how we can provide solutions to each of those areas."

Hold the page up vertically, and use a pen or pointer during the discussion. You need to be familiar enough with the layout of your suite-of-solutions wheel to know where each core offering is located.

This allows you to be able to look at the influencer while pointing to individual items on the document.

When presenting the wheel to your Influencer:

1. Point to the core product or service from the wheel that matches up with the first PITs item that you uncovered in your needs analysis.
2. Briefly review what the issue was, in the terms given by your influencer, to refresh his or her memory and provide the foundation for your solution.
3. Explain what your company can provide to the prospect to address that specific issue.
4. Provide backup documentation as appropriate, such as the letters of recommendation described in Chapter 1, to reinforce your credibility as a valid solution provider for that specific needs area. Other items that would be of value here include product samples, process documentation, and appropriate brochures or marketing literature.
5. Close for agreement by asking a trial-close question, such as "Is this something that you feel would be worthy of inclusion in my proposal?"

At this point, you move to the next PITs item. This process is repeated, one need at a time, until you have addressed each of the opportunities that you uncovered in the needs analysis.

PREDATOR POINT

The suite-of-solutions-wheel is an excellent leave-behind resource. It serves to reinforce the key points that you made in this initial meeting.

A Final Trap to Avoid

Here again, we come to a point where we risk a loss of control of the process. The most common reaction that you will get at this point—and it is a positive reaction, albeit a dangerous one—is to have your influencer ask you for costs or pricing. The absolute worst thing that you can do here is provide it. Keep in mind that this person is usually an influencer, not a buyer. That said, when you give pricing at this point, you are providing this information to a person who cannot buy what you are selling.

Therefore, if pressed for pricing, be polite but direct. Say, "Pricing will depend on a number of factors. However, I will provide detailed pricing information for you in my proposal." If the influencer presses further for pricing information, provide a "ballpark" figure. "It could be anywhere from a minimum of $__ to a maximum of $__ depending on a number of factors; however, I will be able to provide specific figures in my proposal."

A more practical reason for avoiding this discussion is the simple fact that providing pricing at this point is both premature and inappropriate. The conceptual presentation is an informal discussion of capabilities conducted with one person and nothing more. You simply don't have enough information at this point to get into a discussion of pricing. There are other people in the company who will have input on the needs you have uncovered; each of them will have his or her own opinions and views on how these issues affect the business. They may add some new items to the list, and some of the existing items even may be removed. I will discuss who these people are and how to work with them in Chapter 4.

Chapter | 4

ROLE CALL

Identifying the Inner Circle

When we left Chapter 3, we had just completed a detailed needs analysis with our influencer. We explored both public information and private information issues of the company. We presented conceptual solutions to the influencer and explained in general terms how we might be able to be of value to the influencer's organization. We are now concluding what has been, so far, a productive and worthwhile discussion.

As this meeting moves to its ending, we must maintain a leadership role in the competitive selling process. We must have a clear strategy for moving this successful first step forward. We must know where we want to go—and where we don't want to go. And, at this critical juncture, we must avoid a strategic mistake that will be made by most of our competitors.

Seller Beware!

We've already established that your goal for the first meeting, if it goes well, is to secure a second meeting to get the input of the people with an interest in the final decision. Unfortunately, this will not be the objective of your influencer. Not by a long shot.

Following the conceptual presentation, the influencer will ask you for a proposal because this is what he or she has been instructed to do. The influencer's intent is to obtain all competitive recommendations and submit them "upstairs." From the influencer's viewpoint, as well as that of the people that he or she reports to, this is the logical next step in the decision process. It is also the point at which most of your competitors, by complying with this request, will doom themselves to losing the business.

Keep in mind here that when your influencer requests a proposal, you are being asked to give your pricing to a person who does not have the authority to buy. You therefore have no business submitting recommendations at this point, for the simple reason that you have not obtained the input of the other people involved in the buying decision. When you comply with this simple request, the influencer has no further need for your involvement in the process, so you have effectively eliminated any remaining reason for your continued participation.

This point will be lost on your competitors. Therefore, let them comply. Let them submit their proposals and exit the playing field. Your success lies in being the potential vendor who first identifies and then gains access to those who initiated the buying process.

PREDATOR POINT

When asked for pricing by your influencer, the worst thing that you can do is to comply with the request.

This chapter details the roles of these other people. It explains their respective duties with regard to the competitive buying decision. It identifies the roles that each plays so that you can be successful in gaining access to them.

The Inner Circle

When a buyer goes to the trouble of contacting several different options before making a buying decision, this act alone tells you that the decision is significant. It also virtually guarantees that there will be several and often many people within the prospect company who have a stake in the outcome of the decision. I will refer to this group of individuals as the *inner circle*.

The inner circle is the group of people who have responsibility for vendor selection; they are also the people who directed your influencer to get in touch with you and your competitors in the first place. This is the decision team around which the buying decisions involving your product and/or service lines are made. The roster of people involved can vary depending on the specific application, as well as the magnitude of the decision. A good rule of thumb to remember is that the rank and number of people participating rises in direct proportion to the significance and potential impact of the decision.

In most cases, each of these people will be affected to a degree by the selection that is made. This is why each of them is participating. It is critical that you understand the different roles played by each member of the inner circle so that you can then establish a game plan to gain their support for your recommendations.

Company Culture and the Inner Circle

One fundamental question about the prospect company that you will need to consider regarding the makeup of the inner circle is the type of corporate culture in which the group operates. There are two basic types in a competitive sale: the innovator and the replicator.

The *innovator culture* encourages risk-taking and creativity among its employees. This is the company that wants to gain market share. It strives to be the first in its industry with a new service, product, or idea. In most cases, this philosophy carries over to its buying practices and, by extension, to the inner circle. When you are competing for the business of an innovator company, your demonstrated ability to help the company enhance its market share and differentiate itself within its core businesses not only will trump the recommendations of your competition but also will usually make the issue of price a nonfactor in the buying decision. Innovators will pay a premium for good advice, and they welcome unique approaches to addressing business challenges. They are also a lot of fun to work with. The bad news? This corporate culture is the exception, not the rule.

Much more common is the *replicator culture*—the company that follows the pack rather than leading it. The mantra of the replicator is simple: "Let's keep up with the Joneses." Replicator companies will rarely, if ever, be the first company in their business to implement a new concept or idea and prefer instead to watch from the sidelines while an innovator competitor takes all the risk. If that innovator succeeds, then the replicators typically follow suit.

The replicator mentality carries over into the competitive sale as well. Replicators are conservative by nature. These prospects want to know, first and foremost, "Who else have you worked with?" They place a premium on references and will check your credentials carefully if you are viewed as a serious contender for their business. The inner circle for a replicator company will want all vendors submitting proposals to follow strict guidelines as outlined in the request for proposal (RFP), and they usually do not respond well to creativity, such as a recommendation in a proposal that deviates from stated parameters or objectives.

Identifying which culture you are dealing with is important to your strategy for winning the business. When making your initial visit to the prospect, conduct your due diligence. Review the company's Web site and its mission statement. During your visits there, take a hard look at the investment they have made in the building, the furniture, and the technology. Learn as much about the organization as you can. If possible, talk to other vendors in noncompetitive service areas who have worked with the prospect. These activities can tell you volumes about the kind of people with whom you are dealing.

PREDATOR POINT

All companies have one of two buying cultures: innovator or replicator.

The Myth of "Sell to the Decision Maker"

As noted earlier, your entry into a competitive selling opportunity is initiated with a phone call from an influencer requesting a meeting. However, while this is the beginning of the process for you, it actually marks the end of a process for the company with which you are hoping to do business.

The fact is that the decision to buy from *somebody* already has been made by the time you and your competitors have been called into the discussion. Figure 4–1 shows the usual chain of events as follows:

1. Someone in the company initiates an idea or points out a need.

Figure 4.1

How companies initiate most buying decisions.

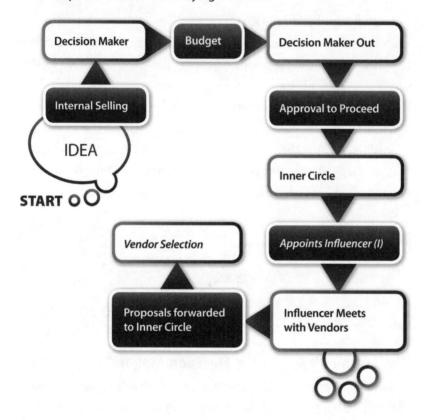

2. This person then "sells" the idea internally to others,
   including his or her direct supervisor. The idea or need is
   validated by this person and at this point receives an official
   stamp of approval for formal evaluation.

3. A group of employees with an interest in the idea—the inner
   circle—is gathered to discuss it. Additional members of the
   group who have an interest or a stake in the idea or need are
   recruited at this point.

4. The idea or need is formalized. At this point it is then formally submitted by the ranking member of the inner circle to the person with authority to approve a budget for it. This, in selling terms, is your decision maker.

5. The decision maker then approves the funding for the idea— giving it life, in a sense—and, having done so, removes himself or herself, completely and permanently, from any further involvement in the process. In other words, since the funds are approved prior to your being contacted, the person who approved the budget is long departed from the scene by the time that you and your competitors arrive for your initial meetings. This is neither good nor bad; it is simply the environment in which you are operating.

This simple point is a critical, and often overlooked, difference between routine selling opportunities and competitive ones. After the funding has been approved, the inner circle now "owns" the budget and has the authority to interview different vendors and make a selection without the decision maker's further involvement. Salespeople who ignore this transfer of ownership and focus on selling to the decision maker are wasting their time when it comes to the competitive sale. They pursue access to a person who has not a smidgen of interest or involvement in the active buying process. They get nowhere, they annoy the influencer, and they are do not get what they really need—input and buy-in from the members of the inner circle.

PREDATOR POINT

In the competitive sale, your target buyer is not the decision maker. Once this person approves funding, they are no longer involved in the buying process. The inner circle now owns the decision.

What You Know—and What You Don't

Our needs analysis with the influencer provides us with a thorough understanding of *his or her perception* of what the company wants. Assuming that you properly covered the steps we have outlined to this point in the process, you know, from the influencer's perspective, where the "gaps" are between the company's current situation and its desired one. This information now serves as both an asset and a liability.

This is so because it is common for your influencer to be poorly informed about his or her role in the buying process. In fact, in many cases the influencer's instructions from the inner circle may be limited to nothing more than "do some looking around and see what is out there." In these situations, your influencer is relying largely on speculation when discussing his or her employer's wants and needs. The influencer is speaking for other people—and, through no fault of his or her own, may be doing an exceptionally poor job of it. To take this information at face value is likely to land you in the same firing squad–style selling situation that I described in the Introduction.

Even in a best-case scenario, you will find that only the primary, or public information, needs of the company will be identified accurately by the influencer. We assume here that these issues were properly communicated to the influencer by the inner circle prior to the initial inquiry. However, even in these cases, the private information (secondary) needs are an altogether different story. Remember that your secondary issues discussion was entirely comprised of questions that the influencer was neither expecting from you nor prepared to answer. Therefore, the private information that you gleaned from the influencer is based on his or her opinions on those issues and not by any means on known facts. Rest assured, the inner circle will have differing opinions on some and perhaps all of these private information areas.

PREDATOR POINT

The influencer's responses to your private information questions are their opinions. These are not validated facts.

An Illustration of the Influencer's Role

Some years ago I was contacted by a sizable Midwestern bank to discuss my firm's training services. My initial meeting was with an influencer who had been directed by a senior vice president at the bank to contact me. The meeting went well; we spent over an hour together in a detailed discussion of the organization and its needs. The influencer explained to me that the bank was looking for a training program specifically designed to teach professional selling skills to its branch managers.

As part of my needs analysis, I learned that the vice president made the final decision and had personally directed the influencer to contact me. The influencer's role, as usual, simply was to meet with me and then provide the vice president with my recommendations in the form of a proposal. In the course of our initial discussion, I asked my influencer for a meeting with the vice president.

The influencer's reply to this request? He was polite and to the point: "No, since I am the screen, and my job is to keep you from talking to that person." Not at all what I wanted to hear and certainly not an action plan that was going to meet my need for gathering accurate information. I had a decision to make: What did I have to lose by ignoring this person's request and going over his head?

Using a technique that I will cover later in this book, I made my decision and went for broke. In this case, I was able to tactfully navigate around this person. I got a detailed summary of my discussion with the influencer in the hands of the vice president. In the summary, I asked the vice president to review the list of key needs for sales training that I had gleaned from the influencer meeting and to let me know if he had any questions or changes.

As it turns out, he did. I received a phone call the very next morning. The vice president was impatient and annoyed.

"Why are you wasting my time with this proposal?" He demanded. "I need a leadership program for my branch managers, not some sales training program." He demanded that I meet with him personally to discuss what he actually wanted, which I was, of course, glad to do—and I subsequently had to completely rewrite my proposal to get the business.

Incidentally, once I was summoned by the vice president, I called the influencer, explained the situation, and invited him to this second meeting.

His apathetic response? "Well, no thanks. I don't really need to be there."

Sometimes, you do what you have to do.

Who You Know—and Who You Don't

Most inner circle buying groups will have, in addition to your influencer, six different buying roles. One person can have multiple roles, and you also may have multiple people in the same role. Each of these six roles will positively or negatively affect your chances of winning the sale. These are as follows.

Vested-Interest Contact

In a competitive selling situation, every inner circle will have one participant who stands to gain (or lose) personally the most as a result of the decision that is made and, by association, from the vendor that is ultimately selected. This person is referred to here as the *vested-interest contact* (VIC).

The VIC is often a midlevel manager—the person in charge of a department, for example—and, as such, may or may not have the final word in the selection process. However, his or her area of responsibility will be directly affected to a large degree by the purchase decision, so he or she naturally has the most at stake. For this reason, the VIC wields a considerable amount of influence within the buying group. Simply stated, if the VIC isn't on board with your recommendation or, worse, likes your competitor better, you have a huge problem because the rest of the inner circle almost always will yield to the VIC's wishes. A no vote from this person in the competitive evaluation process is a virtual guarantee that you will not be selected. It is therefore critical that you identify this individual early in the selling cycle and focus on gaining his or her buy-in as part of your competitive selling strategy. While the VIC cannot necessarily ensure your success, his or her support is a huge asset.

To identify the VIC, ask your influencer: "Whose department or what manager will be affected the most by the option that your company selects for this decision?"

Spock

Even if you have never watched the original *Star Trek* television show, you will be familiar with the two lead characters, Captain Kirk and Mr. Spock. Kirk, as the ship's captain, was the "decision maker" on the *Enterprise,* and Spock was the ship's science officer. As a lower-ranking member of the crew, Spock was accountable to his captain—at least on the organizational chart, that is.

In reality, whenever a crisis or some other significant event presented itself, Spock immediately took over. He had the final say on most important decisions. He would assess the available options and advise Captain Kirk, and Kirk almost always would follow his recommendations to the letter. In other words, Spock essentially made the big decisions in the capacity of a trusted advisor, and Kirk then would execute those decisions. This dynamic was present for one simple reason: Spock's depth of expertise far exceeded that of his ranking officer, and he therefore had an enormous amount of informal power. In fact, to my recollection, there exists not a single episode of *Star Trek* in which Captain Kirk ever overruled or ignored one of Spock's recommendations.

A *Spock* personality is seen often within inner circles. Spock is the person within the group who possesses the most in-house expertise with regard to your products or services. Because of this, he or she will assume a key position of authority and will serve as an advisor to all the other members of the inner circle. He or she also will have an especially strong influence on the VIC—a point that you should take into consideration as you plan your selling effort. Spock's opinion carries the most weight of any member of the team. In fact, most vendor-selection decisions by the inner circle will be made only after receiving Spock's "blessing" to move forward.

One aspect of Spock's personality that you must be prepared for is a large ego. This is a person who is used to telling others what to do and having other people follow his or her instructions without question or resistance. That said, never volunteer your opinion or advice to Spock unless asked for it, and never make the mistake of "showing off" your knowledge base to this person. This tactic usually will blow up in your face. They aren't interested in what you think, and if you attempt to challenge the omnipotence of Spock, you will regret it.

If Spock wants to know your opinion, he or she will ask. Otherwise, you are likely to find that the best way to work with Spock is to assume the same position that everyone else does—one of subservience to the resident expert. Essentially, this means catering to his or her every whim, following his or her directions to the letter, and basically saying, "Oh Great One, how many I serve thee?" Spock appreciates a salesperson who recognizes his or her rightful place in the universe and knowingly bows to a superior intellect. This may not sit well with you and your own inflated ego, but it works—so suck it up and play Spock's game, not your own.

To identify Spock, ask your influencer: "Who at your company is the resident expert regarding [whatever your firm provides]?"

The Trigger

Customers want competitive firms to believe that the inner circle operates as a single decision authority—as in, "Our committee will be making the decision." This is nonsense; in my experience, when it is time for the group to make a "committee decision," everyone on the committee looks down the table at one person. The group waits for that person to speak. That person then says, "I think we should go with _____." Everyone else enthusiastically nods in agreement. "That is exactly what *I* was thinking." So much for democracy in action. Every inner circle has its *trigger*.

The trigger is the person who has formal authority for approving the recommendation of the inner circle. This person may or may not be the ranking person within the group. He or she is the de facto decision maker once the budget is approved, as outlined earlier. He or she "owns" the budget from the moment it is approved and will make the vendor selection official after the committee completes its assessment of options and makes its recommendation. The trigger ultimately can choose whichever option he or she pleases and can even override the entire group's selection if he or she chooses to do so.

In my experience, this almost never happens. In case you haven't figured it out already, Spock is frequently, but not always, the person who serves in this capacity.

To identify the trigger, ask your influencer: "Who owns the decision?" or "Who has final approval authority?"

PREDATOR POINT

When meeting with the inner circle, validate the group's position on key issues with the trigger.

The Mole

I was once involved in a large selling opportunity with a well-established manufacturing firm. This was a unique situation in that some years earlier I had lost a sale at the same company to a competitor. In the time that followed, that decision had not worked out to the company's satisfaction, so I found myself with a second chance to win the company's business. This time I was much better prepared. This time I asked for and obtained access to the inner circle.

For this second chance, the decision process was different, and it had a much larger cast. The new group consisted of 12 key personnel—a tough crowd filled with large egos. It was the classic example of "too many officers and not enough soldiers." There were lively exchanges and even some heated arguments. It seemed that everyone had his or her own agenda. I knew which person played the role of the trigger, but otherwise, the clash of personalities made it difficult to discern who was influential, who wasn't, and what role each person played in the decision process.

Fortunately, I had a *mole*.

One of the members of this inner circle had worked with me in a previous life at another company, had been pleased with the results, and wanted me to win the business. Because of my prior relationship with her, she proved to be invaluable in helping me to do just that.

At my initial meeting with the inner circle, the trigger publicly informed me that the committee would be looking at several of my competitors. Yes, I expected that. Then my mole pulled me aside during a break and whispered excitedly, "Guess what? Your firm is the only option we are considering!"

Well. That was nice to know.

At our second meeting, the trigger also told me, again publicly, to sharpen my pencil—that cost would be a significant factor in the group's buying decision. The mole pulled me aside during a recess in the discussion and casually asked me, "Would you like to know what the budget is?"

Yes, I replied. As a matter of fact, I would. Very much.

We eventually got to the proposal stage and—surprise!—this second time around I won the account.

Now you understand the value of having a mole.

Having a mole in the competitive sale is the single biggest advantage you can hope for. This is a person who wants you to be the winner—and therefore is motivated to work proactively to influence the other members of the inner circle in your favor. As in my case, the mole will share information with you that you aren't supposed to have—and he oe she will advise you on how to best deal with the other members of the group. The mole will tell you what your competitors are up to, who within the inner circle is hot for one of your competitors, who supports you, who doesn't, who is trying to stab you in the back, who doesn't care either way, and a host of other interesting tidbits that make all the difference in a competitive selling environment.

Unfortunately, the example provided—where you have a mole preestablished from the outset—is exceptionally rare. However, this does not prevent you from developing a mole relationship within the prospect company. The mole can be anyone within the inner circle— but you are looking for a person who makes it clear that if it were his or her sole decision, you would be the selected vendor.

What motivates someone to be your mole—to work with you as a partner in the competitive sale? Liking you personally is a plus, but that alone is rarely enough to make the person become the kind of proactive ally that you need. For this relationship to bloom, you will need the right circumstances. Examples:

- Prior knowledge of your firm, either from a prior experience or, more commonly, through word of mouth from a friend or colleague
- A poor experience with one of the competitors involved or a negative report from a friend or colleague
- A perception that your firm is uniquely capable of serving his or her personal interests in the decision
- The perception that your firm has an offering or strength of particular significance to the needs of the company
- A dislike of another member of the inner circle who is leaning toward your competition, with a corresponding desire by your mole to scuttle this person's "getting his or her way"

As you begin working with the group, pay close attention to who among the group seems to gravitate toward you. Select a mole candidate, and work to align yourself with this person. Address his or her "What's in it for me?" and develop a proactive partnership that yields benefits for both of you.

PREDATOR POINT

The mole is the single most valuable asset you can have during the course of any competitive sale.

Outliers

Depending on the complexity of the opportunity, your inner circle may lack expertise regarding the decision being made, or you may have people in the group who simply want to reduce their personal risk with regard to making a poor selection. In either case, they sometimes decide to include an outside firm that will be contracted by them to render an objective opinion on your and your competitor's capabilities. I have served in this capacity on a few occasions. Such independent firms most often participate as "Spock for hire" in this capacity, and they usually will have a well-established relationship from prior dealings with the company. I will refer to these hired advisors as *outliers*.

Outliers behave, for all practical purposes, just like Spock does, with a twist—they first and foremost want to use this opportunity to impress their client with their expertise. In fact, this is just one of several political angles that outliers may work within the competitive buying decision. Consider the situation that I outline below.

I recently had a worst-case scenario in which I found myself dealing with an outlier who had a separate agenda from the buying decision. A man who owned several different but related business units was interested in my services. He had a close relationship with a consulting firm, one on whom he relied heavily for advice in the other business units. What the owner did not know, but I did, was that this outlier from the consulting firm had a very close and formal business relationship with a competitor of mine who also was being considered. The owner made the assumption that his outlier could be of value in objectively assessing outside resources, not knowing that the outlier favored my competitor. I knew better. In fact, as soon as the discussion began, I realized that this entire process was going to be a complete waste of my time. The outlier had hand-picked his buddy to get the work. I was an unexpected interruption to that formality, chosen to be there by a separate senior executive, and none of my firm's value-adds were going to matter one bit in what the outlier recommended to the client. Faced with the choice of exposing this political power play to the buyer or removing myself from the process, I elected, in the interest of time management, simply to "punt." I informed the decision maker that I did not feel that I was the best fit for this particular application and moved on to other, more productive uses of my selling time.

Drones

Aside from triggers, Spocks, moles, and outliers, there can be other members of an inner circle who were recruited to participate, although their interest level in the outcome may be limited or even nonexistent. Their role is therefore a peripheral one. I refer to these individuals as *drones*. I will discuss such secondary participants in more detail in Chapter 5.

Drones, in most cases, will act as passive members of the inner circle. For a variety of reasons, it may not be in their interests to take an active role in the decision—and they therefore will serve primarily as observers.

Some examples of drone participants include

- A member who has a highly specialized skill or expertise relative to your offering and therefore is asked to sit in as a special guest

- A member whose previous career experience included time with a company that sold the same or similar things that you and your competitors do
- A protégé of Spock or the trigger who is being groomed for promotion and therefore is participating as an observer for the learning experience
- A valued assistant, such as an executive secretary, who is routinely included in these decisions based on demonstrated business acumen, tenure, and good judgment

A common mistake that sellers make with drones is to assume that their job title or role in the company reflects their role in the buying process. Don't make this mistake! One of the most important inner circle players in one of my key accounts is the secretary of the executive vice president; her opinion is a key factor in all major buying decisions. Keep your eyes open, and get to know everyone. You will be able to determine from observation most of the key players within this group.

PREDATOR POINT:

Don't assume that a person's role in the competitive selection process is automatically reflected in their job title.

Knowing what the different roles are within the inner circle is a complex challenge. An equally important, and related, aspect of working with this group is understanding the role of office politics in vendor selection. In Chapter 5 we will take a look at how these different members of the inner circle interact with each another—and with you.

Chapter | 5

GAMES PEOPLE PLAY
Politics in the Competitive Sale

The dictionary defines *to play politics* as follows: "to deal with people in an opportunistic, manipulative, or devious way, as for job advancement." In the competitive sale, this perfectly describes the behavior of some inner circle members, with one minor modification. It's you, the salesperson, who can expect to be dealing with opportunistic, manipulative, and devious individuals as you navigate the competitive selling process. Exactly what does opportunistic, manipulative, and devious look like in this environment? Consider the following example.

Why Politics Matters

In my first "real" sales job, I sold dictation equipment for a large office equipment company through its Dallas, Texas, office. Although I was new to sales, I made up for my bumbling presentations and general lack of business skills with old-fashioned hard work. In my case, this meant lots of door-to-door cold calls in the tall glass office towers of north Dallas.

One afternoon, my foot-canvassing forays landed me, without an appointment, in the office of a senior partner of a large law firm in the city, an outfit employing over 100 attorneys. If you are familiar with the intricacies of the legal profession, you know that lawyers use massive amounts of dictation equipment. That being the case, I was delighted to gain some "face time" with this gentleman.

On this particular call, the partner had invited me in from the reception area for the purpose of discussing an immediate need for replacing the firm's entire outdated inventory of dictation equipment (hallelujah!) This was an opportunity that, if handled successfully, would provide me with a commission check exceeding my meager income for the entire previous year. Needless to say, I could not believe my good fortune.

He then took me on a tour of the office so that I could see what his people were using, which turned out to be the product line of my arch-rival competitor. I suggested that I take a complete inventory of the entire office so that I could provide a proposal to replace everything that the firm had.

"Wait, I have a better idea," the lawyer responded. "Why don't you let us try your products across our office for 30 days on a trial basis, and let us compare the performance of your equipment line with the ones we currently use. In the meantime, bring me your proposal. If we like the way your equipment performs and the price is comparable, we will replace everything we have with your stuff."

I was more than happy to present this request to my sales manager and told the attorney that I would follow up promptly. We shook hands on this agreement, and I left. I also should note here that this was the last direct contact that I ever had with my new "friend."

I went back to my management team and was immediately given the green light to pursue this opportunity. As I had been instructed,

I arranged an appointment with one of the administrative staff at the law firm to set up the trial. I then spent an entire day and a half crawling around in the ceiling of their offices as I ran cable across both floors and set up dictation stations for everyone to use. Over the course of the next 30 days, I visited the office several times a week. Everything was performing perfectly, all the employees were delighted with what I had provided, and I had begun making plans for what to do with the impending windfall soon to come.

At the end of the agreed-on 30 days, I called for the partner's decision. His secretary called me back. The response I got was short and to the point: "We need another 30 days."

I went to my management team with this request, and they agreed to the extension.

On the fifty-eighth day of the trial, I got my "answer." It turned out that a decision had been made. Specifically: My "prospect" had taken my product list, obtained my existing in-house competitor's current product list, made a phone call to that competitor, and placed an order for every comparable item that I had quoted, right down the list. He then had his secretary call me, this time to request that I come by and collect the equipment that I had placed on trial. The competitor who got the sale never even made a presentation to win the business; he just took the order over the telephone. When I went back to the office to pick up all the equipment I'd provided, I found myself riding the elevator, side by side, with the competitor who had received the benefits of all my hard work. He was there simply to get a signature on his sales contract.

That was one long elevator ride.

The buyer in this case never had a serious interest in changing vendors; he saw an opportunity to get two months of free usage of our products at no cost, and he simply took advantage of my youthful enthusiasm and inexperience. In other words, he was a predator of a different sort. He was a Judas, one of the political personalities that we will examine in this chapter.

Nobody ever said that competitive selling is fair; this is just how the game of business is played sometimes. Since you, too, may be dealt such cards in any competitive situation, your best approach is to understand the motivations of the people who are dealing the cards and have a sound strategy for playing whatever hand you receive.

Politics, as we all know, is a part of doing business. Politics in competitive sales, however, is played at a different level entirely. Because choices are being made among multiple options, the value of political capital to those involved carries a higher premium than in most other business situations. Members of the inner circle, including your influencer, all have a single bottom-line concern that overrides every other factor regarding buying decisions: "What's in it for me?"

This chapter examines some of the most common political issues that influence competitive sales, as well as the personalities of the people who propagate them. I also will discuss ways to work with these different personalities to achieve your desired outcome—winning the business.

What Motivates Political Behavior?

In a competitive selling situation, you should recognize that members of the inner circle will gravitate toward making competitive vendor choices based on criteria that serve their own interests first and therefore are not necessarily objective. In other words, their reasons for selecting one vendor over another may have little to do with that competitor's relative strengths and everything to do with serving some personal agenda of the individual making that choice. Common examples of these reasons that you may encounter include

- A predisposition to stick with an existing supplier who hasn't been meeting expectations, but has the loyalty of an inner circle member who wants to retain him or her
- A fear of losing influence by having the company partner with a different vendor—one that has strong ties to a rival member of the inner circle
- A fear of being made to look incompetent by a well-put-together salesperson who has the technical expertise and people skills to expose that person's lack of knowledge of ability
- A financial benefit or "perk"—for example, tickets to sporting events—that a member of the inner circle stands to gain by selecting one vendor over another
- A personal friendship/relationship with or loyalty to a competitive supplier

PREDATOR POINT

In a competitive selling situation, always remember that personal interests will trump company interests when making business choices.

The Eight Politicians of the Inner Circle

Political behavior in competitive sales is exhibited in one of eight distinct and different ways. Let's take a look at each of these personality types and how to deal most effectively with each of them.

The New Sheriff

A familiar theme in western movies is the arrival of the new sheriff, the rugged individual who arrives on the scene to "clean up the town." The same character role can exist within the inner circle as well. In a selling opportunity, the *new sheriff* will be an individual who has been promoted recently to a position of responsibility, such as management of a department or business unit. In competitive selling situations, this is most often a newly appointed department head or perhaps the leader of the task force charged with making a new vendor selection. In most cases, the person is full of enthusiasm owing to his or her newly acquired power, and his or her first order of business is to make changes—to "clean up" the department. This giddiness wears off after a period of time, but in this case, that hasn't happened yet. As the person evaluates where changes need to be made, a presumption he or she usually makes is that any condition that existed prior to his or her arrival is automatically tainted simply because it was part of the old regime. It doesn't matter whether it was a good situation or not; the mere fact that it existed previously is sufficient cause for changing it.

New sheriffs therefore become an asset or liability to your sale depending on how they view your ability to help them to implement change. Because of their desire to "shake things up," they deserve special attention during your needs analysis work. This can work to your benefit in a big way if the new sheriff has marked your existing-vendor competitor for inclusion in the cleanup effort. If you can demonstrate an understanding of the new sheriff's vision for this area of responsibility, he or she can be your strongest ally when it comes to new vendor selection. This is one politician that you should pay special attention to when conducting your inner circle interview. Ask your influencer if there have been any recent promotions within the inner circle group.

PREDATOR POINT

Understand, and align yourself with, the vision of the new sheriff. They can become your most enthusiastic advocate.

The Lap Dog

I recently completed a stint on the board of directors of an organization at the behest of the board president. I immediately realized why: This individual knew that I would unconditionally support whatever efforts she wanted to accomplish as board president. All her initiatives had to be approved by majority vote; there were people involved in the decision process who opposed her, and she therefore was having difficulty in getting some of her objectives approved. That is where I would be an asset. Although never stated, I was fully aware that my dependability in providing a needed vote for her agenda was the primary reason that I was asked to join the board in the first place. In other words, my role was that of *lap dog*. Since I happened to fully support her judgment, I was perfectly happy to be her toady.

To gain leverage for their views on vendor selection, it is common for senior members of the inner circle to employ the use of a lap dog as well. In the competitive sale, this is an underling of one of the senior members whose sole function is to unconditionally support whatever the boss wants to do. Lap dogs therefore are drafted. They are essentially a "bought vote" for whoever pulled them into the decision process. They skew the playing field, providing an unfair advantage to those who use them by increasing the influence of the ranking member to whom they swear their unfaltering loyalty.

In your meeting with the inner circle, the lap dogs usually will be seated next to their masters. They rarely speak their own mind; they will wait for the boss to introduce a topic or question to you, and then they'll "bark" with follow-up inquiries of their own, the main purpose being to demonstrate support for the person who asked the initial question. The important thing to remember about lap dogs is that their "owners" have the real power in the decision process—by having skillfully garnered at least two votes for whatever they decide to support. Focus your selling efforts on gaining buy-in from the lap dog's master, and the lap dog will follow.

The Spineless Wimp

I once had a meeting with a local company—one with whom I had initiated contact—to discuss ways in which I might provide value to its sales organization. This topic of discussion yielded little opportunity for us to work together, but as a courtesy, at the end of the meeting I asked the group if they had enough interest in my services to warrant my preparing a proposal. Instead of simply responding appropriately—by saying "No"—the trigger responded by asking me to submit a proposal to him for a completely different matter—a possible customer-service project. This request was a "curve ball" to say the least. It's an area in which I do very little work because I specialize in working with sales forces. At any rate, I accepted and subsequently presented my recommendations directly to the trigger. I included references from two of the small handful of clients for whom I had performed similar projects.

At the end of my presentation, I asked him for his reaction to my recommendations. The trigger thought for a moment and then responded with yet another request on top of the earlier one: "Could you provide me with additional references?"

This was, of course, a reasonable next step—provided that the company had a serious interest in hiring me. However, I had by now,

become jaded and had reached the conclusion that this endless ban-
ter wasn't headed toward the destination I wanted. Putting together a
list of references would require additional work on my part. I needed
to know that the extra effort would be rewarded.

So I decided to be direct, answering his question with a question of
my own: "I would be happy to provide you with additional references.
However, if I do so, and they provide a good report to you, are we
ready to move forward with this project?"

You might interpret this question as being "pushy." I beg to differ. My
time is valuable, too. The answer I got was exactly what I expected—
and, in this case, wanted.

"Well, we just can't make that commitment at this time" said the
trigger.

"Why don't we do this, then," I replied. "Let's table the reference
issue for now, and when you are ready to move forward with this project, let me know, and I will provide the references you need at that
time. How does that sound?"

"Sounds like an excellent idea", said the trigger with a big smile.
We shook hands and parted company. That was nearly eight years ago.
I am still waiting for that request for more references.

You might think that I was disappointed with the outcome of this
situation. Actually, I was delighted with it. You see, my trigger was a
spineless wimp—a very nice person who was so nice, in fact, that he
could not bring himself to say "No." This type of inner circle member will always want you to invest additional time on some useless task
so that he or she can postpone the unpleasant task of delivering bad
news. By bringing the issue to a head, I saved myself a couple of hours
of wasted time—and since the spineless wimp wasn't willing to stop
wasting his own time, I made the decision for both of us. My "win"
here was avoiding putting together references for an opportunity that

did not exist and was never going to happen and moving the time saved to a productive task.

In a competitive sale, spineless wimps are pleasant, passive individuals who strive to avoid conflict at all costs. They will defer to others during your needs analysis questions and rarely offer an opinion of their own. Their primary mission in life is simple: "Don't rock the boat." They maintain a position of neutrality throughout the decision process and can be easily swayed by the more dominant personalities of the inner circle.

Your strategy with spineless wimps is to maintain their stance of "not saying no." In other words, since they will go along with whatever the rest of the inner circle wishes to do, your best approach is to avoid stepping on their toes, keep them in their current state, and focus your persuasion efforts on the people who are leading the selection process.

PREDATOR POINT

With some inner circle members, maintaining a state of neutrality is the best position that you can achieve—and is often an adequate outcome.

The Whine Enthusiast

It was my first day of work at a new job—one that turned out to be the best experience of my life as a salesperson in the corporate world. I had just been hired as a sales representative for the large and very successful southeastern office of a national industry leader, and I was excited about my new opportunity. My first morning there only reinforced that I had made a very good career decision. I was escorted around the entire building, introduced to all the department heads, and generally made to feel like a valued and important part of the team. I returned to my gleaming new cubicle full of good cheer and optimism.

That's when I got my first visit from Barry the Whiner.

Barry, as it turned out, sat directly in front of me in the sales department. Barry was more of a distributor than a salesperson. He would acquire bad news, problems, and other depressing tidbits; place them in the invisible garbage bag slung over his shoulder; and then redistribute those products among all who could be persuaded to listen to him. During my tenure there, I noticed that every new hire in the company received a visit from Barry the Whiner as part of his or her orientation process; on this particular morning, it was my turn.

"So, has anybody told you what it's *really* like to work in this place?" inquired Barry with a knowing smirk and arched eyebrow.

"Ummm, gee, no, Barry," was the only response that I could muster.

"Well," he started before pausing to peer over the top of my cubicle to ensure secrecy. Then he settled into the other chair in my workspace, folded his hands, and leaned forward. "Let me tell you exactly what you've gotten yourself into."

As he began his review of why I had just made a heinous career decision, I came to the realization that this was less of an educational experience than a recruitment speech. I was being interviewed—tested, really—for membership in his "Whine Enthusiast Club." Barry, as it turned out, led a small but devoted group of followers—a cult, really—who shared his negative view of the world and everything in it. While it turned out that I didn't fit his requirements for membership, future new hires occasionally did, and they perpetuated the mission of all "whine enthusiasts": dutifully casting a veneer of want and woe over everyone and everything with which they come into contact.

Whine enthusiasts are a royal pain to everyone involved in the buying decision. They focus on finding something—anything—wrong with whatever you, your competitors, or their inner-circle peers propose. If they cannot find something wrong, they will find a way to make it up. In short, they are very creative at creating problems.

Salespeople tend to overact to the negativity exhibited by this person. They try too hard to please a person who cannot be satisfied, and this behavior serves to give the whine enthusiast a spotlight that he or she does not deserve.

Your best strategy with whine enthusiasts is patience. Recognize that other members of the inner circle are used to their melancholy ways and therefore assign them little credibility. Stay neutral. Answer their objections. Don't feed their thirst for drama by becoming defensive or, worse, rattled by the points they pursue. In other words, be boring to them. Eventually, they will become bored with you as well. They will soon throw in the towel if their efforts at creating problems for you yield little in the way of tangible results. Let your competitors tangle with the whine enthusiast. Focus your efforts on meeting the needs of the people who want to get something positive accomplished.

Judas

Judas, as the name implies, is a person who feigns support for you while enthusiastically stabbing you in the back. This politician is, first and foremost, the ultimate opportunist. He or she will gladly throw you (and anyone else, as necessary) under the bus, without hesitation or remorse, to attain a desired goal or objective.

One particular Judas was a peer I worked alongside of as a saleperson. He was a nice enough guy and, to all outward appearances, was everything that he made himself out to be. This perception was tainted somewhat, however, the day that several of his peers, including me, noticed accounts on his monthly new sales report that resided in our sales territories, not his.

To salespeople, this is commonly known as *poaching*—selling business that does not belong to you. (Outside the sales profession, this is known more commonly as *stealing*.) The issue was sent up the chain of command in our office, and on being confronted with the evidence, our Judas tearfully copped to his crime.

"Forgive me," he pleaded, and just like the real Judas, he was forgiven but never trusted again.

In the field of competitive sales, the phrase "Buyers are liars" was coined for these individuals I describe as Judases. They will misrepresent their true intentions without hesitation to achieve their desired outcome. They will tell you that you have their sole endorsement, when, in fact, they have made identical statements to the other vendors involved. They will promise you that your recommendations will be kept confidential and then immediately provide complete copies of your proposal to all your competitors. They will tell you that your price is the highest of the options being considered, when, in fact, you are the least expensive one on the table. In short, they will say and do whatever is necessary to accomplish their personal agenda.

How does one deal with a person with such low ethical standards? Your only savior with a Judas is to employ the services of the mole. Remember that your mole is a person who will help you to navigate the political minefield of competitive selling. Ask your mole for feedback on who your friends and foes are. If there is a Judas among your inner circle, your mole will know. He or she will identify the Judas for you—and provide you with an action plan for dealing with the problems that he or she creates.

PREDATOR POINT

The mole is an invaluable asset to have when coping with the more devious people that inhabit the inner circle.

The Lockhorns

One of my largest clients has two members of its inner circle who simply cannot tolerate one another, and they cannot be in the same room without arguing constantly. When one has an idea or suggestion, the other immediately opposes it—often for no other reason than the pleasure of starting a debate. In fact, no matter how petty the issue, if one speaks up, the other immediately chimes in, always to disagree. A spirited exchange invariably ensues, and the rest of the group sits back to be witness to the carnage. That's the interesting thing about the *lockhorns*—once they get started, you as the salesperson become a spectator, along with the rest of the people in immediate proximity. Meetings involving these people tend to resemble the *Jerry Springer Show*. The end result is always the same—neither side wins, and once the hostilities cease, both are silent until the next opportunity for disagreement presents itself.

The worst thing that you can do with lockhorns is to insert yourself into their fray. Their need to disagree has nothing to do with you—so, unless you are asked your opinion, your best strategy is to stay out of it. If one attempts to drag you in, be careful with your answer—you cannot offer an opinion supporting one without alienating the other.

As with the whine enthusiast, maintaining neutrality with these people is your best strategy.

The Pouncer

The *pouncer*, like a lockhorn, enjoys confrontation—except that the target is not a peer. The target, instead, is you. These people are ambitious, driven, and aggressive. They want attention, and they are preoccupied with making an impression on their peers within the inner circle. Their methodology is to dominate the discussion by asking intentionally pointed or difficult questions designed to put you back on your heels.

The worst pouncers are always those who try to use this venue to impress a higher-up. For example, I once conducted a needs analysis meeting with a room full of data analysts as part of a sales-development project. The company wanted to give these employees a basic education in the fundamentals of professional selling. All these individuals were peers of one another. They each had the same job level and responsibility, and not a single one of them had ever been in sales. It was evident to me from the outset that most of these people were not terribly interested in becoming sales champions, let alone learning how to sell, period. Most were meek, and the group was largely quiet. I had two or three individuals who were answering all my questions for the entire peer group.

That all changed dramatically when a door in the back of the room opened and a small, elderly gentleman—the CEO—quietly entered. "Never mind me," he said quietly as he took a seat in the back of the room. Few of those present bothered to heed that advice. Rather, they all appeared to be vying for his approval.

Instantly, I was peppered with questions—some of which, it is worth noting, were among the most pointless I have ever been asked—as this group of neophytes suddenly played a game of one-upmanship with one another in an effort to garner brownie points with the CEO. It was difficult to conduct a meeting in an atmosphere of such noisy zeal.

A few minutes later, as is often the case, the CEO departed the room. Instantly, the demeanor of the group changed back to its original level of timidity and reserve. I ended up winning the account and subsequently found the people present that day to be a pleasure to work with. It was a curious departure from the behavior they exhibited the day that a brief opportunity for political gain unexpectedly presented itself.

When confronted with a pouncer, your best strategy is to use what the great sales trainer Tom Hopkins calls the "porcupine technique"—answer their questions with questions of your own. Be polite and patient, but press for details. Respond to their initial attacks with "Can you elaborate on what you mean?" or "Can you be more specific?" Note that each time you do this, the pouncer will be drawn further and further out on a limb in full view of his or her peers. This is an uncomfortable position for most people to be in, and in most cases, the pouncer will quickly back off. The exception—and a real inner circle challenge in the competitive sale—is when you have a Spock (resident expert) who is also a pouncer. In this case, you are dealing with a power player who can go as far out on that limb as you care to and will relish the opportunity. If you can determine ahead of the meeting that you have a Spock-pouncer hybrid, bring your own technical support expert to the meeting with you. He or she can be an invaluable asset in handling this person's aggressive interview style.

PREDATOR POINT

When dealing with a Spock/pouncer hybrid, don't go it alone. Bring in your own team of experts to back you up.

The Sniper

Of all politicians in the competitive sale, the *sniper* is the most dangerous of all. This person, a "cousin" of Judas, is a master of behind-the-back sabotage. While Judas pretends to be your friend, the sniper makes no effort to be friend or foe. Snipers are, in a word, sneaky. At least pouncers play fair. If they disagree with you or have an issue with an aspect of your proposal, they will let you know about it. The sniper never extends that courtesy. The sniper operates behind the scenes to undermine your success.

If you've ever lost a competitive sale that you thought was a "sure thing" and never found out why you lost, you were probably a sniper victim. Snipers lay in wait; they sit quietly during the entire course of your inner circle discussions, never challenging any point that you make, never asking any questions. They appear for all intents and purposes to be completely benign. What they wait for, patiently, is for you to leave so that they can attack unimpeded, when you have no opportunity to defend yourself. There are a number of reasons they do so, but their reasons are irrelevant. What is important is that you are aware of the threat so that you can do something about it.

To neutralize a sniper, you must first identify him or her. In addition to assistance from your mole, another tactic that can be highly effective is to watch body language—specifically, eye contact. People who won't look you in the eye when you talk directly to them should make you nervous. Study them. If you feel that you have a potential threat looming—enough, in fact, to warrant addressing it—below is an aggressive yet subtle tactic that will take your sniper out at the knees.

Neutralizing the Sniper

At the end of your meeting with these people, you will—as covered in Chapter 6—want to verify that there are no remaining issues or concerns that you have not covered. Let's assume that you think that Jane, one of the participants, is a sniper threat.

First, ask this question of the group: "What other issues do you have that I have not addressed?"

Then look directly at Jane and say, in front of everyone, "Jane, you've been quiet so far. Do you have any issues or concerns that you want to address?"

Jane, true to sniper form, will say, "No."

Immediately move on. Look at the rest of the group and ask one final time whether anyone else have any final concerns. Nobody will.

Then proceed with the conclusion of the meeting.

You know what they say at weddings: "Speak now, or forever hold your peace." You just gave sniper Jane a public opportunity in front of all her peers to address any concerns that she had—and she publicly declined your offer. Now, if she attempts to attack you after you have left, you can see the situation you have created. The rest of the group will say, "Why didn't you bring any of these issues up when you were asked?" Jane will have a problem that she cannot solve. She then will back off from her mission of sabotage, and you will have neutralized the threat.

Now you know that the key to dealing with politicians is to first understand what motivates them. At this point, you are prepared to engage the inner circle for the first time. In Chapter 6 you will learn how to get that face-to-face meeting with these people.

Chapter | 6

FACE TIME

How to Gain Access to the Inner Circle

Now that you understand the political gamesmanship of the inner circle, the natural next challenge is having an opportunity to actually talk to these people. Getting the green light from your influencer to interview this group is the last formal step in the initial meeting. It is also a step that is not likely to be pursued by your competition. To get this accomplished, it is important to first look at the issue of granting access from the influencer's perspective.

Influencer as Gatekeeper

The influencer has a number of reasons—and, from his or her point of view, perfectly sound ones—to keep you from having access to the inner circle. These commonly include

- "I might lose control."
- "You might upset somebody."

- "I could be perceived by my superiors as being incompetent."
- "I can handle this myself."
- "If I let you have access, the other vendors will want it too."

PREDATOR POINT

The influencer's reasons for denying you access are completely legitimate to them, and must be respected.

If you put yourself in the gatekeeper's position, you can see that all these concerns are understandable, irrespective of the fact that they may be without merit. Keep in mind that influencers are risk-averse people. They want to handle the task assigned to them properly, they don't want to "rock the boat," and they want to avoid making mistakes. You cannot blame them for assuming an initially conservative position with regard to the access you desire. You can, however, change their mind. What is needed is a reason for you to have access that effectively trumps all their reasons to deny it. Fortunately, you have one.

Why Should They Allow You Access?

Your reason for needing this access is always preestablished and valid. It has nothing to do with you wanting to win the competitive sale — and everything to do with your responsibility to the company to which you are selling. Your first obligation to any customer is not to win a sale over your competition; it is to help that customer to make a well-informed business decision. This point supplies the validation for your request: You cannot meet this obligation unless you have input from anyone in the company who has a vested interest in what you will be recommending.

What you face here is a flawed decision process on the part of your buyers that prevents them from making a well-informed business decision. In other words, trying to propose solutions based on the input of just one person—your influencer—is not going to meet this requirement, nor will it result in a proposal that addresses the concerns of the other people involved. This point is not a cheap-trick sales gimmick to wheedle a meeting with the inner circle. It is simply a commonsense fact that, if presented properly to the influencer, should give you the access you need—and deserve.

Another factor that comes into play here is the issue of trust. It goes without saying that your influencer's decision to allow you access will be heavily based on how you have conducted yourself thus far in the meeting and whether he or she trusts your judgment. Here again, following the plan outlined thus far in this book will pay dividends. By properly establishing rapport, following an agenda, and conducting a spot-on needs analysis, you will have built credibility and trust with your influencer.

Five Steps for Gaining Access to the Inner Circle

So now we arrive at the point where the influencer will ask you to prepare a proposal. This is your *cue*—the moment at which you must take action. You have two choices here: You can either agree to this request, which is what your competitors will do, or you can suggest an alternative approach. Since you have no business providing a proposal to someone who does not make the buying decision, let's take a look at a better, alternative plan of action.

Step 1: Change the Subject

It is worth noting that in any conversation, the person asking the questions controls the conversation. So, at the time that the influencer asks you for a proposal, he or she is in a position of control. This situation needs to change. You need to temporarily assume control of the discussion by asking a question of your own—one that will move the discussion, for now, off this topic. Rather, at this point in the meeting, you should return the conversation back to your conceptual presentation—a review of ways in which your firm might provide value.

Simply say the following: "If we set the proposal issue aside for the moment, how do you feel at this point about my company's overall ability to meet your needs?"

This is the perfect question at this juncture. The influencer will respond to it with a statement such as, "So far, I like what I have seen." His or her response to the question, as long as it is not negative, is unimportant. What is important is that as of this moment you are no longer discussing your submitting a proposal to the influencer. You are now discussing value rather than the price of producing that value. You have, in effect, changed the subject.

With this issue addressed, you now move the conversation in a completely different direction. Your next task is to identify the target group—the inner circle—that actually will be making the vendor selection decision.

Step 2: Identify the Members of the Inner Circle

Your choice of words is critical when you ask what can be perceived as a sensitive question. Remember that your "gatekeeper" here is risk-averse. If he or she feels threatened by any of your questions—or if you are too direct in asking them—he or she is less likely to cooperate with you. Simply asking who will be making the decision therefore is not the best approach in addressing this delicate subject.

To bring up the issue of the inner circle, present the question to the influencer in this manner: "In selecting a vendor for this project, what does your process normally entail, and who else besides you will have a role in that process?"

In most cases, the influencer will respond by rattling off titles—"Our vice president of operations, our marketing manager, etc." Once the influencer completes the title list, he or she usually will provide more information if asked for it. You need more information. Follow up the first question by now requesting names:

- "And who is your vice president of operations?"
- "And your marketing manager?"
- "And your plant engineer?"

Finish up this portion of the discussion by asking one final question: "Which of these people has final ownership of the decision?"

This person is your trigger.

PREDATOR POINT

Knowing the titles of the inner circle members is not sufficient. Knowing "who" means knowing names.

I once had the opportunity to ask this question during an initial meeting with the trigger present. In this case, during the phone inquiry, I had asked my influencer for—and was immediately granted—an audience with the inner circle for my very first meeting. After presenting my agenda, I asked two questions.

First: "Is there anyone else involved in your decision process who is not present today?"

No, there was not.

Second: "Who here has final ownership authority for your decision?"

Six fingers immediately pointed to a woman sitting directly across from me. With this knowledge in hand, rest assured that I paid special attention to everything that she said during the course of the meeting. In short order, I won the account.

Step 3: Asking for Access

Once you know who is involved in your buying decision, you will need to provide a sound reason for obtaining a meeting with them. Remember what I said earlier: Your strategy with the influencer is one of collaboration, not evasion. Except in special circumstances, which I will review later in this chapter, you will not be well served by an attempt to go around the influencer to reach the other people. You want to partner with your influencer. To accomplish this objective, present the request for access as follows:

> It has been my experience that these other people will have different questions and concerns with regard to my firm's capabilities.
>
> With this in mind, as a next step, I would like to request a second meeting to include yourself and these other people prior to my submitting a proposal. At that time, I will review what you and I have discussed, answer any further questions that they may have, and make sure that I completely understand everyone's concerns.
>
> This will ensure that my recommendations are the best possible fit for your company's requirements.
>
> Can you assist me in getting this meeting scheduled?

Obviously, you are going to get one of two outcomes to this request—"Yes" or "No." If you follow this material to the letter, you can expect to be given the access you seek, initially, about 50 percent of the time—and with practice and the conviction that comes from knowing that this is in both your and the other party's best interest, you can expect your success rate to "top out" at 65 to 70 percent.

This still means that a healthy number of influencers are not going to allow you the access you need. So what? Get over it. You cannot dictate the influencer's reaction to the request, so you do not control that variable. You are always going to have people who say no to you, irrespective of how skillfully you may have handled these steps.

Your job *is* to execute the steps properly. If you do this, enough of your influencers will say "Yes" to make the ones who say "No" a nonfactor in your overall success. However, you do need a fall-back strategy for handling "No," and I will discuss how to do that in a moment. First, let's consider what you can control, which in this case means what to do when your influencer says "Yes."

Step 4: Moving the Process Forward

When you get a "Yes" to the request for access, you must take a leadership role—immediately—and outline for your influencer how to make this next step happen. Take charge of the situation by saying the following:

> Great. As a next step, let me give you several dates that will work for my return visit; check with your group and let me know which of these options will work best for everyone. [Provide three different dates and times.]
>
> Following our next meeting, I will return to my office and prepare a customized proposal that will reflect everyone's input on what your company is requiring for your decision, and finally, after my proposal is completed, we will schedule a third and final meeting, at which time I will make a group presentation.
>
> How does this approach sound to you?

This will sound like an excellent suggestion to your influencer, because your plan of action makes perfect sense. You are also making this entire process easy for him or her by organizing the steps to make it happen. Also note the term *group presentation* as it is used here. Your presentation meeting, to come later, will be with all the members of the inner circle. You have "bundled" a group presentation request into your presented plan, and it is being approved with the rest of the agenda. This single factor virtually guarantees your selection, for reasons that will be explained later.

PREDATOR POINT

Take a leadership role in moving the process to a next step. This makes it easy for your influencer to say "yes".

Step 5: The E-mail Introduction

Once you have approval to proceed, ask the influencer for the e-mail addresses of the inner circle members, and explain to the influencer that you would like to send a brief e-letter of introduction to each person *after* the second meeting has been scheduled. Then, once the meeting is formally on the calendar, e-mail each inner circle member. Thank them for their willingness to meet with you, and ask them to reply with any specific issues that they would like to discuss in the upcoming group meeting. Do this step about 48 hours before the scheduled discussion. It is a shrewd, professional touch that sets the tone for a productive session later.

Implications for Success

Just how important is this second meeting to your success in winning the competitive sale? To answer this question, consider the factor of your *close ratio*—the number of sales closed over the number of proposals submitted.

The average business-to-business (B2B) close rate for salespeople is about 15 percent, meaning that for every seven presentations made, the average salesperson gets one yes and six nos. If you analyze, as I do, what actually takes place in these lost opportunities, you will find that most of the nos result from presenting recommendations to influencers and not getting input from inner circles.

In my experience, if you can successfully gain access to the inner circle, interview those people, and make your later presentation to that group, your close ratio increases to—are you ready for this?—75 percent. In other words, for every four presentations made, you will get three yeses and one no. This is a 500 percent improvement in your close ratio—with very little additional work. This is a huge factor in winning competitive sales—more important, in fact, than anything else that you do during the entire process. The old adage, "Who you know is more important than what you know," is true after all.

PREDATOR POINT

Gaining access to the members of the inner circle improves your chances of success by five hundred percent.

Implications for Your Competition

You might assume that if you are given access to the inner circle, your competitors automatically will be given this access as well. My experience has been that in actual practice this is rarely the case. The reason is simple: These are busy people. Because of your approach to the issue, they may have time to meet with one vendor—you—but unless the other competitors involved learn of your success and then request a group meeting, it is not likely that they will be offered it. The inner circle simply does not normally want to take the time to meet in this fashion with everybody. In most cases, if you are successful in gaining access, you will be the sole vendor who does so. This means that you effectively shut the door behind you as you move the process forward—leaving your competitors on the other side of the door.

Figure 6.1 shows how this process typically unfolds.

As this figure shows, you and your competitors all have your initial meeting with the influencer (*i*). The influencer asks all three of you to submit proposals directly to him or her. Your competitors comply immediately. By doing so, they formally remove themselves from the decision process. You ask for—and receive—access to the inner circle using the material presented earlier. Following this second meeting, you come in a third and final time to present your proposal personally

Figure 6.1

How to outmaneuver your competition.

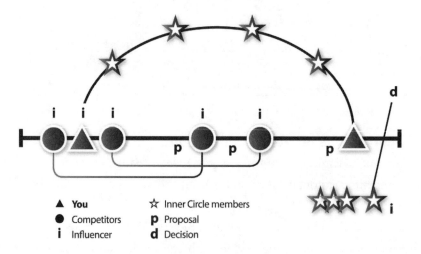

to the inner circle—and are the only vendor that does so. The decision for the inner circle essentially becomes a contest between two paper proposals and a face-to-face interaction with you.

This isn't fair. But who said life—or selling—was fair? The fact is that this process virtually guarantees you the business. It reduces your competitors to nothing more than passed-along documents, whereas you are the only option that "took the time," from the perspective of the inner circle, to delve into what the group truly wanted.

Some years ago I had this exact experience from the buyer's side. My business, located at the time in the Midwest, had grown to the point that I could live pretty much wherever I pleased, and my wife and I decided to move our family, and my business, back to the Carolinas, where I am from.

Since we were in no hurry to sell, I decided to try to sell our home myself. We had a lot of interested buyers but no offers for the first few weeks. Then the need to sell took on urgency because we found a home that we wanted to purchase. So I began looking for a realtor.

At least half a dozen agents had contacted us by this point, so my wife selected three to interview. Two met with my wife but not with both of us because I was traveling. The third, however, had a different approach.

"When would be a good time for me to meet with both you and your husband?" this agent asked.

"It will be very difficult to do that because he is traveling quite a bit right now," my wife replied.

He was persistent—and he finally succeeded in scheduling an introductory meeting with both of us.

The three of us met one Saturday morning at our kitchen table. This agent was young—31, to be exact—but his sales skills belied his age. He began by telling me that I was asking too much for my home.

I laughed, "You guys always say that."

"Well, let me show you," he replied. He then spread a map of our neighborhood across the kitchen table, with the final sales price noted for every home that had sold in the last 18 months. In short, in the space of about two minutes he showed me that he was, in fact, absolutely correct—our asking price had, indeed, been too high to attract a serious buyer.

"What do you suggest, then?" I asked him. He produced a detailed marketing plan and stated that if we would be willing to lower our asking price by about 7 percent, he could find a buyer in short order. We did as we were told, sold the house for the price we were asking within two weeks, and moved to the Carolinas.

I learned later that this young man was the top-producing real estate agent in the entire city in which we lived—but we did not know that at the time we listed with him, nor was it a factor in our decision. What made my own decision easy was three choices that I had available—two brochure packets from his competitors and our face-to-face meeting with him. Given those options, it was no contest. Once again, the ability to secure a meeting with all interested parties carried the day.

When the Influencer Says "No"

It goes without saying that you are not always going to get what you seek. Even if you execute the steps outlined earlier to perfection, you are going to have plenty of influencers who simply will not want to cooperate with your request. This message will be communicated in a variety of ways; some of the more common ones include

- "That won't be possible; they are all too busy."

- "If I let you talk to them, I would have to let your competitors do the same."
- "I am fully capable of handling this myself."

In each case, your influencer is entitled to his or her point of view. What can, or should, you do in such situations?

You can either throw in the towel or you can try a fall-back strategy that will still accomplish your goal: Appeal to the influencer's risk aversion.

Your influencer sees risk in allowing you access. What about the risk to your influencer of taking sole ownership for handling vendors and collecting proposals? Specifically: What if the information that he or she filters and forwards to the inner circle produces a decision that turns out badly—does he or she really want to take sole responsibility for this potential outcome? This is a real and valid issue that influencers will rarely contemplate unless it is raised by you. You can, and should, raise it under these circumstances before giving up on your need for access.

To raise this point, say the following to your influencer:

> If you want to handle this on your own, I am happy to work with you in any capacity that you like. However, I do know from experience that if I do not get input from the other people involved in this decision, two things are likely to happen here:
>
> First, the proposal that I submit will not be well received by the others in your decision process because they had no input on it.
>
> Second, and more important, the likelihood of your company being dissatisfied with what you ultimately select is higher because I am working here with information from just one person.
>
> Because of these factors, I suggest that we go ahead and schedule a second meeting before I create a proposal. How would you like to proceed?

PREDATOR POINT

Handle a "no" to your request for access by appealing to the influencer's aversion to risk.

After this statement, let the influencer respond. Some influencers will see the wisdom in your suggestion—namely, that they can spread the risk of making a bad decision around by including the inner circle from its inception—and acquiesce to your request. Others will stubbornly adhere to their position. In either case, you have nothing to lose by bringing up this point; it is a valid one. Try it, and see how they respond.

Fall-back Strategies

Depending on the circumstances, there are sometimes situations where you may consider going over the head of your influencer. These situations must have a unique condition that makes doing so a no-lose proposition—in other words, you should have virtually no chance at winning the business any other way before proceeding. In such cases, as the old Jesuit saying goes, "It is better to ask forgiveness than permission." Some of these situations can include the following:

- *Complexity.* Complex decisions involving extensive data require that your influencer must be exceptionally well versed in the company's needs and issues. If this is not the case, you are wasting your time in pursuing the business in this manner.
- *The level of your influencer.* Some influencers have more influence than others. A vice president or higher-level

influencer has considerably more clout than an assistant—and this has a direct impact on their ability to sell or not sell on your behalf.

- *Your relationship with the influencer.* A cooperative partner is a valuable asset; an antagonistic stonewaller is a hindrance to both you and the business that employs him or her.
- *An entrenched incumbent is your competition.* In this scenario, what do you have to lose? If you have a competitor already in the company as an entrenched incumbent, then the answer is "Nothing," and the decision is made for you.

Now that you know the potential circumstances—those where your influencer is a serious impediment to you doing your job—here are some options for how you may consider dealing with the problem:

1. *Write a letter.* This is the option I used with the bank whose influencer informed me that "my job is to keep you from speaking to the decision maker." Summarize the initial meeting with your influencer in a cordial letter or e-mail to the powers that be. In your correspondence, bullet the points that you understand are of key importance to the inner circle. Ask your contact(s) to review the list and e-mail you with their comments or questions. Then hold your breath and hope that your inquiry triggers a response. What you are counting on, of course, is that there are issues of importance to the other people that were not discussed in your initial meeting and therefore are not listed in your documents. This scenario causes an inner circle member to initiate contact with you and ensures that these points are included. On having this initial discussion with the inner circle member, you suggest that a second meeting is in order.

2. *Drop in unannounced.* This is a more brazen tactic, but it works. Go by the place of business, and bring your needs analysis information from the initial meeting with you. Have a specific member of the inner circle as your target. When you walk up to the front desk, tell the receptionist that you are working on a pending proposal for the company and have a couple of questions for your target contact regarding issues that were discussed in the previous meeting. If you are successful in getting a sit-down with this person, reference these points and ask for his or her input on them. If the meeting goes well, suggest—again—that a second fact-finding meeting with the other members of the inner circle would be a good idea. This person has the power to promptly make it happen.

3. *Refuse to participate.* This is another "gutsy" approach. Out of the three options, this one has the least likelihood of success— but it's entirely appropriate if you have a low chance of winning otherwise. Simply tell the influencer that you don't feel comfortable proceeding with a proposal that doesn't have the input of everyone who has a vested outcome in the recommendations you'll be making. Then wait for him or her to respond. If the company considers your firm to be a highly desirable vendor, this may be enough to sway your influencer to your way of thinking. If not, so what? You probably avoided wasting a lot of your valuable time on an opportunity that you weren't going to win regardless.

PREDATOR POINT

Don't go over the head of your influencer unless you have nothing to lose by doing so.

Recognize that by following any of these strategies, you are going to alienate your influencer and potentially derail any chance that you have for winning the account. Make sure that you are involved in a situation where the risk is worth this potential penalty before proceeding.

Irrespective of whether you get your inner circle meeting through a collaborative relationship or with one of the preceding alternative approaches, once you do get it scheduled, you must have a plan for managing this event.

Structuring the Inner Circle Meeting

The ideal scenario for your inner circle meeting would include the ability to meet with each person in the group on a private, one-on-one basis. This is so because, in a group dynamic, some inner circle members may refrain from "opening up" in front of their peers. If you can secure a series of one-on-one meetings with your inner circle group, by all means do so. I will assume here, though, that time constraints will limit your access to a single meeting with the entire group, which usually will be the case.

The Second Meeting Agenda

As you did with your influencer, you will want to use an agenda to establish your goals for this meeting. After all, you asked this group to meet with you, so they will be expecting you to make good use of their time.

Following the agenda structure that we used in Chapter 2, an appropriate agenda for this meeting follows:

Thank you, everyone, for taking the time to meet with me today. Here is what I would like to accomplish:

First, I would like to review the information that _____ provided me in my last visit to your company so that I can make sure that we are all on the same page.

Next, I would like to get your input on some ideas that I shared with _____ for addressing these issues.

Finally, once we have covered these items, I would like for us to get a date and time scheduled today that is convenient to the group for me to present my formal recommendations at a later time.

How does this sound to everyone?"

The response you will receive is, "That's fine." Now you must proceed with the review of issues that were discussed with your influencer.

How to Review Influencer-Stated Needs

When reviewing the minutes of your initial meeting, separate the public information and private information items into two separate groups, and review the public items first.

Reviewing Public Information

When going over the public information needs:

- Review your understanding of each issue, one at a time, as it pertains to their business. Be as detailed as possible.
- After reviewing each item, ask for confirmation from the group that you appear to understand the issue completely and accurately.
- Ask the group if anyone has anything to add before moving on to the next item.

In most of these situations, the inner circle members will chime in with their opinions on one or more of these public information issues. This is precisely what you want because the information shared with you here is not being distributed to your competitors. Pay close attention to what you are told, note the role of the person sharing the information, and take excellent notes. These comments will play a key role in the development of your later proposal.

Reviewing Private Information

The private information issues are covered next—and delicately! Keep in mind that these are issues that were the sole opinion of the influencer. None of these issues were provided as part of the request for proposal (RFP), and they need to be validated by the group before you assume that they are indeed relevant. Don't present these items as facts; test the water first by introducing them for discussion:

Don't say: "My understanding from [the influencer] is that you also have problems with _____."

Do say: "As part of our first meeting, [the influencer] and I discussed several additional areas of your business that were not included in the RFP. I would like to get the group's input on whether or not you feel that these items should be addressed in my proposal. Would this be okay with everyone?"

PREDATOR POINT

Do not present private information needs as understood facts when introducing these points to the inner circle.

Once you get a "Yes"—and you will—introduce each of your private information issues, one at a time, for discussion. Again, when doing so, don't repeat what the influencer said. Instead, tell the inner circle, "It was my understanding that you may be having some issues with _____, specifically, _____. What can the group tell me about this part of your business?" Note how you remove the influencer from being accountable in the way you phrase the question. Never put your influencer in a position to feel threatened when bringing up issues; this is an ally and a partner that you want to protect when introducing what amount to potentially sensitive topics with the inner circle.

Wrap-Up: Closing for the Proposal Meeting

At the conclusion of the meeting, confirm that you have covered all your bases by asking this final question: "What other issues have we not discussed?"

If anyone raises a surprise item, address it. Otherwise (and assuming that you have no sniper to deal with), move the meeting to closure. Ask the group to get out their calendars and — while you are still there — get the appointment for presenting your recommendations set with the group.

PREDATOR POINT

Always set the appointment for the group presentation while you are in your first meeting with the inner circle.

Once this last step has been accomplished, you can thank everyone for their time and head back to your office — knowing that you have the information you need to prepare an excellent proposal. Remember, though, that you almost always will have competitors submitting proposals as well. In Chapter 7 we will discuss how to eliminate those competitors from consideration.

Chapter | 7

THE PROCESS OF ELIMINATION

Removing Competitors from Consideration

Competitive selling is not so much a game of winning as it is a game of avoiding elimination. Your buyers are on a quest for the ideal solution provider—the option that best demonstrates an ability to address their needs. To find it, they will, from the outset, begin stack ranking competitors against their desired outcomes. No one vendor will be a perfect choice; all will have perceived strengths and weaknesses with regard to the expectations of the inner circle. The "winner" therefore is the last one left standing after the other options have been discounted.

The Winner Is the Last One Standing

The choice of one vendor over another does not wait until the end of the selling cycle. In most competitive sales, buyers will use a two-tiered assessment process to decide their final selection. The first of these two steps—and the one that we will focus on here—occurs before the proposal stage and usually immediately after the needs analysis. It involves a "paring down" of the initial list of potential vendors by eliminating, outright, any who do not meet one or more key criteria established by the inner circle. In other words, vendors who are perceived after the initial series of meetings as lacking a basic deliverable are often removed from consideration. Even if they remain "in the hunt" following that conclusion, these competitors are at a severe disadvantage as the decision process moves forward. This conclusion is reached as the result of one of two scenarios: Either the inner circle determines this deficiency as a result of its own internal due diligence or an outside third party brings the issue to their attention by introducing that variable into the mix.

PREDATOR POINT

The inner circle will quickly eliminate competitors that are perceived as lacking in key requirements.

Keep in mind that to winnow out any ineligible vendors, the inner circle will rely on whatever information it has at hand when making that decision. This creates a significant opportunity for the dominant predator who understands how to *tactfully* leverage this selection dynamic. If you can create the perception that an impartial issue raised by you is important to the overall selection process, and it is brought to the attention of the inner circle that one of your competitors is lacking in that area, you may be able to eliminate that competitor from further consideration. We will discuss how to do this in detail later in this chapter. First, though, to bring such issues into the decision process, you have to be aware of them.

How Well Do You Know Your Competition?

Dominant predators know their competitors' strengths and weaknesses as well as they do their own. They relentlessly seek out and compile information about the culture, people, capabilities, existing product lines, new products, organizational changes, technology, and service offerings of their rivals. In short, they know their competitors almost as thoroughly as if they were employed by them. They also know how each of their rivals sell—and especially how their rivals sell against them. They may use a variety of resources to collect this information, but no source approaches the value of a loyal customer who has experienced first-hand what your competitors say and do in the competitive selling process.

In the best-seller *Good to Great,* author Jim Collins advises us to focus on improving our strengths, not on shoring up our weaknesses. This superb advice has great relevance in competing with other vendors. By learning what you do well in the competitive sale, and by doing more of it, you will gain much greater competitive leverage than by spending your time improving an area that is not one of your strong points.

The place to find out what your competitive strengths are lies, first and foremost, within your customer base. In fact, the *only* people who can accurately tell you what you do better than your competitors are your customers. If you aren't finding out directly from these people what your strengths are, you may *think* that you know, but you have not validated your perceptions. In other words, without customer feedback, everything that you accept as fact is based purely on speculation. Therefore, go to the places of your past victories—the customers who chose you after evaluating you and your competitors—and interview them. If you want to find out where your competitors do not meet your level of value delivery, this is, hands down, the place to do it.

PREDATOR POINT

Your client base is the only place to learn what your competitive strengths are.

How Well Do You Know Yourself?

Much is made about finding out why you lost a sale. Finding out why you *won* a sale is 20 times more important to know. Every time you win a competitive opportunity, you must ask these three questions, in this order, as soon as you are awarded the business:

1. *"What was it that I said or did that led you to choose us over your other options?"* What could be more important for your future success than learning this information? The answer that you get will tell you what your competitive strengths are. This answer is the single most important fact that you can glean from each "win." Focus on doing more of whatever they tell you in every future competitive sale.

2. *"What did you like and what did you not like about the other vendors that you were considering?"* This will tell you volumes about both your competitors' relative strengths and weaknesses as they are perceived by your prospect; the information that you get will be almost as good as if you had been present for your competitor's meetings with the buyer. Learn what your competitors tout as their competitive strengths, and research those statements to validate (or invalidate) their claims. We will put this information to good use in a format that we will discuss later in this chapter.

3. *"What did the other vendors tell you about our firm that you found relevant or interesting?"* This will reveal each competitor's

level of professionalism, confidence, and aptitude when competing against you for business. You will learn how they sell against you—and provide you with the ability to counter their tactics in advance of future opportunities.

Case in point: After winning one such competitive opportunity as a salesperson, I got to this third question—I asked my new customer what my competitor had said about my employer. This particular competitor was a salesperson with a much smaller firm—and a rep whom I had been running into on a regular basis. The customer shared with me what he had been told about us, and I quote: "Their firm has thousands of customers. If you do business with them, you will find yourself a very small fish in a very large pond."

In future competitive sales opportunities, I used this tidbit against him—I would actually quote him in my initial meetings. Without naming names, I would tell the prospect, "We are the largest provider of our service lines in this market. Because of this, one of the things you are likely to be told by other vendors is that if you buy from our firm, you will find that you are—I think they use the phrase—'a very small fish in a very large pond.' I would like to take a moment to address why we are the most popular option in the marketplace, which is a testament to the personal service that we provide each client."

I then would preempt the pending attack by addressing the issue directly. Imagine the scenario that my competitor then would walk into when the potential customer would chirp the phrase "very small fish in a very large pond" as he began his meeting with these prospects. This tactic served to do more than simply negate the bad-mouthing effort made by my competitor. It also showed the buyers that I knew my competition intimately and enhanced my credibility. Both these points worked in my favor.

The Issue of Pecking Order

In Chapter 6 I outlined an effective strategy for securing a second meeting with the inner circle, where by doing so we are also able to extend the decision process to our benefit. If our competitors submitted their proposals, as requested, to the influencer, then we—by gaining access to the inner circle—also virtually guaranteed that we would be the last vendor to present our final recommendations. There is no question that when it comes to this step of the competitive process, being the last vendor on the schedule is the choice place to be.

Does this same logic apply to the earlier phase of the competitive sales cycle—conducting the needs analysis? Is it better to be the first or last competitor to have an initial meet with the influencer and, subsequently, with the inner circle? Or does early positioning really matter in the competitive sale?

To be sure, it matters—but that "choice" position may not be what you expect.

Conventional wisdom maintains that in the competitive sale, the least desirable position in the order of competitive sellers is that of the first one to meet with the buyer(s). The logic dictates that the first competitor to enter the competitive selling process has three distinct disadvantages:

1. Whatever you say and do as the first person in will be buried and forgotten during the subsequent meetings with your competitors.
2. You cede to your competitors the ability to adjust and restructure sales strategy based on what the other vendors are doing.
3. You do not have the opportunity to defend yourself against claims made against you by your competition.

These are all valid points, but they wrongly assume that a level playing field exists among the different vendors—and that all competitors will follow the same playbook. Dominant predators change this dynamic. They follow the strategy outlined in this book, and they throw the playbook out the window.

In the competitive selling process, these strategies distinguish you from your peers. When you don't play by the same rules as your competitors, you set new rules for everyone else to follow. When you follow a different and superior strategy than the rest of the pack, you set a higher standard—one that the buyers then will look for from all your competitors. Because of the fact that we are using a refined process to differentiate ourselves from our competition, our objective is to establish a benchmark for the other vendors. Therefore, the preferred position of the dominant predator is to be the first vendor to meet with the buyer(s).

PREDATOR POINT

When beginning the competitive selling process, ask to be the first vendor in.

The Advantage of Being First

When you implement the concepts covered in earlier chapters of this book, there is one major advantage to being the first vendor to meet with the prospective account. It is the ability to set a bar for your competitive followers that is nearly impossible to meet.

This outcome is especially relevant when it comes to the issue of demonstrating results, as discussed in detail in Chapter 1. Whenever you present evidence of your ability to deliver value, recommend to your contact that he or she ask for similar proof of performance in his or her subsequent vendor meetings. For example, when discussing the subject of staff qualifications—the expertise of the people who work at your firm—present your biography sheets to the buyers, and make this statement: "Any vendor that you consider will tell you that they have excellent people. Here is a biographical summary of our staff. If you do decide to partner with our firm, these are the people who will be responsible for ensuring your satisfaction with the quality of our work. I would recommend that you ask for similar documentation from any vendor that you consider so that you can get an accurate idea of the level of service you can expect."

Because your competitors likely will not have such documentation available (in some cases, they won't even know what your buyer is talking about), they are immediately at a significant disadvantage. Because you provided documentation on your staff and your competitors did not, the message of "value differentiation" is loud and clear.

This tactic should be standard operating procedure when you are the first vendor in: point out the importance of each differentiation factor, provide your proof-of-performance documentation, and then explain to your contact that he or she should expect comparable evidence from all other vendors.

PREDATOR POINT

When presenting documentation of results, recommend that your buyer ask for equivalent resources from all vendors being considered.

The Well-Educated Buyer: Your Best Asset

As an experienced professional, you are an "insider" within the industry in which you work. As such, your knowledge base of the key factors that are important for a good business decision usually will exceed that of the inner circle, sometimes by a wide margin. Here again, remember that the inner circle will evaluate competitive offers based only on the information they have available. You therefore can have an enormous influence on the outcome of competitive selling situations by educating your buyers on criteria that are relevant to their selection process.

Consider the example that I cited earlier about the speaking business: Most people who hire speakers for sales-related topics are not aware that a significant number of people who market themselves as "sales experts" have never actually *been* in sales. By educating my clients on this point, I help them to make better business decisions. I provide them with relevant information that they would not have known otherwise.

Relevant does not simply mean criteria that persuade them to buy from you over the competition. *Relevant* here means objective, useful information that assists your buyer in the overall selection process; whether that selection ends up being you or one of your competitors is secondary. In other words, to be deemed valuable, any data that you provide must maintain a level of objectivity within the parameters of the decision. The focus of your educational effort must first and foremost be to provide information helpful to the selection process and not simply to attempt to persuade the buyer to choose you.

Bad-mouthing: To Do or Not to Do?

Is speaking negatively about your competition a wise move? Buyers sometimes think so; they may even encourage this behavior. As one example, I have a speaking-industry peer who tends, owing to his personality and delivery style, to elicit a strong reaction from audiences who see him. Let's just call him Mike. For some people, the reaction to Mike is strongly positive; for others, it is strongly negative. In either case, on numerous occasions I have been asked my opinion of him. "What do you think of Mike?" they ask.

My response is short, to the point, and will always be the same: "Mike is a superb marketer." All of us in the speaking profession have our individual personalities and methods for sharing content; who am I to render an opinion on another individual's delivery style? Mike, in my honest opinion, *is* a superb marketer: talented, funny, and intelligent. He has worked hard to attain his success, and he has a loyal following. Beyond that, I have nothing further to add to what I view as a topic that is best addressed by his clients, not me. I think I can speak for Mike here when I say that he would respond to such a question about me in a similar manner.

Even when not prompted by the buyer, the temptation to bad-mouth the competition can be too strong for some salespeople to resist. In fact, most salespeople assume that the only way to educate buyers on their competitors is to say negative things about them. After all, if you are aware of any additional product, service, or level of quality that you can provide and that your competitor cannot, doesn't it make sense to bring such issues to the attention of those making the choice of vendor? Many salespeople seem to think so. They feel that sharing negative information about a competitor is perfectly acceptable as long as it is considered relevant to the decision process. The outcome of such tactics, however, is always the same, as the following example illustrates.

Bad-mouthing Example: Dastardly Dan

Some years ago I had a direct competitor whose ethics were so low that he would have gleefully sold his own mother out to win a competitive sale; there was simply no level to which he would not stoop to claim a victory. Competing against such an ethically bankrupt salesperson was always an unpredictable and exciting experience. At the time, the company I worked for was the leading provider of business-to-business (B2B) services in the local marketplace, with about 5,000 clients. My competitor and nemesis—let's call him Dastardly Dan—worked for the number two provider; his firm had approximately 3,500 customers in the area.

One thing for which I must grudgingly give credit to Dastardly Dan was his unabashed creativity. There were times when he was worthy of a standing ovation for being so ingeniously underhanded. And of all the dirty tricks that Dastardly Dan had up his selling sleeve during our competitive clashes for business, his master stroke was the use of a reference list—one laden with a sinister and highly effective twist.

For this particular ploy, Dastardly Dan went on a recruiting mission within his company's customer base. He was looking for a small but carefully selected group of his customers who had all been customers of my employer at one time or another. They had apparently endured, for whatever reason, an unsatisfactory experience, which made them essentially hate us. Following the end of their relationship with my employer, they had gone to the "dark side." They had migrated to Dastardly Dan's company, where they now resided as clients.

These firms then were personally contacted by Dastardly Dan. He asked each of them if they would be willing to provide, on request, a comparative opinion to prospective buyers on our respective capabilities. When a customer agreed to participate, he or she was placed on what Dan described to buyers as a "client reference list."

You can see where this is going. When competing with our company, Dastardly Dan would bring his list of "references" out. He would say to the potential customer: "Don't take my word for it that we provide better service than your other option. Here is a list of people who used to be with their firm and are now with ours. They have tried us both! Why don't you call these people so that you can learn for yourself what the *real* differences are between our firms?"

Of course, any prospective customer who picked up the telephone got the same disturbing story—that we were a horrific vendor to work with and that Dastardly Dan's company was a much better choice. Underhanded and unfair? Absolutely. Effective? Very much so—at least initially. In fact, the first few times that I ran into this situation, I was caught completely off guard. "Explain this to me, sir!" one prospect demanded. "I called the people on this list that your competitor gave me, and every one of them says that your company *stinks*!" I left with my tail between my legs.

Fortunately for me, at the time I reported to a team of bright and very skilled managers. I presented this diabolical scheme of Dastardly Dan's to them, and they soon came up with a counterstrategy to defeat my nemesis.

The next time that a prospect pulled out the "reference list," I had my sales manager with me. This is how he deftly handled it:

> Ms Prospect, we have over 5,000 clients, the vast majority of which are happy with the services we provide. When you have the number of customers that we do, it is inevitable that there will be a handful that, for a variety of reasons, may have had a less than exceptional experience with us.
>
> If it would help you in your decision process, we would be happy to provide you with an equally long list of customers who used to be with Dastardly Dan's company, had a poor experience there, and are now with us.
>
> However, my question to you is this: If we provide you with a list of Dastardly Dan's former customers who are now with us, and Dastardly

Dan provides you with this list of our former customers who are now with him, how is this information going to help you to make a good business decision between our two companies?

This tactic, as it turned out, was highly effective. By raising the issue of Dastardly Dan's business ethics, we eliminated the problem. The buyer thought for a moment, admitted that he saw our point, and then we moved on. Most subsequent buyers behaved in the same way to this logic. We immediately began winning most of these competitive situations. Shortly thereafter, Dastardly Dan abandoned this strategy for his next sneaky caper.

PREDATOR POINT

Never badmouth your competition—even when invited by your buyers to do so.

What Bad-mouthing Tells Your Buyer

What Dastardly Dan failed to realize—and what many other salespeople don't take a moment to consider—are the negative messages that you communicate regarding yourself and your company when you make the decision to "put down" a competitor. To illustrate, I'll address this issue as a business owner who regularly sees salespeople and represents the position of most of your prospects on this subject:

First of all, it is extremely unlikely that I will look on any opinions of your competition that you share with me as useful information. The fact of the matter is that unless I tell you otherwise, I am not remotely interested in your input regarding your competition or their capabilities. That assessment is my job, not yours. I also would expect any input that I receive from you on this subject naturally to be skewed, exaggerated, and of questionable accuracy. In short, I prefer that any conclusions that I reach about competing vendors be done without your direct input.

Second, the simple fact that you feel compelled to talk negatively about another vendor labels you as insecure, unethical, and amateurish. I called you into this discussion to help me solve a business problem, not tell me about the lack of service that you feel your competitor provides. Such unsolicited input runs counter to your being a valued business advisor.

Third, and most important, I will reach only one conclusion about your motivations for bad-mouthing your competitor: You must be afraid of them. Your competitor must be good at what they do; otherwise, you would not have been motivated to talk about them. So the effect of your bad-mouthing effort has had exactly the opposite effect of what you expected. You see, I interpret your comments as nothing more than petty jealousy. By saying negative things about your competition, you have now elevated their status in my selection process. They have become a favored option simply because you have seen fit to lavish so much attention on them.

So yes, the message here is to never bad-mouth your competition—even when invited to do so. This conclusion may lead you to feel left between the proverbial rock and a hard place. You cannot speak negatively of your competitors, yet you know that there are areas in which you are clearly superior to them. What is needed, then, is a way to educate your buyers on these relevant issues without stooping to bad-mouthing.

Fortunately, you have one.

The Key Items to Consider List

The most effective and credible way for you to educate your prospects is to remove yourself from the education process and give them the opportunity to educate themselves. This introduces the issue of objectivity into their due-diligence efforts. A tool that I have developed to accomplish this, which is called a *Key Items to Consider List,* is an absolutely lethal weapon for eliminating your competitors from consideration.

The Key Items to Consider List is, first and foremost, a neutral discovery tool for your prospects. It does not have your company name anywhere on the document, nor does it list any of your competitors by name. If structured correctly, it is a useful guideline for evaluating multiple options and, as such, will be welcomed by your prospects. Of course, the key items to consider here will all be strengths of yours—ones that your competitors either cannot match or do not do as well as you do. This allows you to go after your competitors without bad-mouthing them. Your objective is to educate your buyers on your competitive strengths and your competitor's deficiencies without personally inserting yourself into that comparative assessment. A sample—and one that I have used successfully in my own business on a number of occasions—follows.

WHEN SELECTING A SALES SPEAKER ...

KEY CONSIDERATIONS FOR A GOOD BUSINESS DECISION

Owing to market demand, in recent years there has been a significant increase in the number of speakers offering sales-related topics to meeting planners. Because of low barriers to entry, virtually any speaker can proclaim himself or herself a "sales expert." The result? In the current market, there are many individuals presenting themselves as authorities on the subject of professional selling who have themselves never held a job as a B2B salesperson.

In evaluating your options, the following criteria will help to ensure that you choose a qualified, proven resource who has the knowledge and expertise to deliver a valuable and well-received presentation for your audience.

Look for "blended" delivery. Your audience will measure the value of any business speaker that you choose on three key criteria: Take-home value/content, clarity of message, and humor/storytelling ability. The best content experts use a combination of these three resources to provide an experience that is funny, memorable, and provides significant take-home value. Blended delivery is a learned skill. Ask for a video of your speaker candidates, and look for high levels of value in all three areas.

Ask for documented proof of qualifications. When selecting a subject expert, practical experience is both a credibility factor and the primary determinant of value to the audience. Where did your speaker acquire the expertise that will give your people quality take-home value? What accomplishments can he or she point to as proof of his or her knowledge base? Ask for a written summary of the person's formal qualifications for presenting material within his or her claimed area of expertise.

Do your homework—you might be surprised at what you find. A sales speaker whose selling accomplishments are exceeded by those of most of your audience members is not likely to be credible or effective, particularly when taking questions.

Look for a high rehire rate. In our business, the best indicator of talent is the speaker's rehire rate—in other words, what percentage of the speaker's clients have asked him or her to appear more than once. When reviewing past engagements, consider the number of clients you speak with who have had the speaker as a guest on multiple occasions.

Ask for references, and check them carefully. Any speaker can provide you with two or three people who will say something positive about his or her delivery. Ask for a more extensive list that will allow you to call whomever you please—this will give you a much more accurate assessment of the individual's skill level. When interviewing references, the following questions will prove useful in selecting the best choice for your upcoming event.

QUESTIONS TO REVIEW WITH REFERENCES

- What did the client reference like most and least about the presenter's style and content?
- What was the speaker like to work with? Was he or she easy or difficult?
- How would the client reference rate the speaker compared with other presenters who also have spoken to the group?
- How relevant was the material presented to the audience's needs?
- How customized was the material to the audience's needs?
- And most important, what was the feedback received from the audience members regarding the quality of the presentation?

Your decision to select a speaker should be based on a proven track record of delivering outstanding audience value. Audience members today place a premium on information that can be implemented immediately on the return to the workplace. By selecting a speaker who has consistently demonstrated excellence in these areas, you will be assured of a memorable program that serves as the highlight of your meeting or conference.

Creating Your Own

When creating your own Key Items to Consider List, structure is important. Note the following items related to the layout of the document:

1. The title—"When Selecting a _____"—refers to the type of service and/or product that you and your competitors provide to the marketplace.
2. The subtitle—"Key Considerations for a Good Business Decision"—speaks to the impartiality of the text. In other words, we don't say "Key Reasons to Select Me" here.
3. The introductory paragraph discusses general market trends. This should be a brief overview of relevant issues affecting your industry and provides the foundation for highlighting specific items that are of interest to your prospect(s).
4. Each key point is shown in bold type.
5. A paragraph follows each point explaining its relevance in the buying decision. This is absolutely critical—you must explain the "why" aspect of each item that you present for consideration because this is where the prospect becomes educated on the points that you are bringing to his or her attention.

6. A brief list of recommended questions to ask when talking with references is provided. This tactic is a double-whammy for your competitors. Not only are you providing your prospects with questions that will expose your competitors' weaknesses, but also keep in mind that you will be providing a reference list of 25 to 30 names for this purpose, which will be above and beyond what your competitors provide.

As you can see, the items on the list are composed of areas that are relative strengths—in my case, these are based on feedback that I have solicited from past clients, just as we discussed. Therefore, to cite one example, I never have to bad-mouth one of my competitors who lacks practical sales experience. I simply let the prospective client ask that competitor the question, "What career sales experience do you have?" and then draw his or her own conclusions from the response. The result that I desire—that the competitor is eliminated from consideration—is usually achieved, yet I never have to resort to pointing this fact out about any particular competitor myself. In fact, because the prospects learn this skills omission without my direct involvement, it has significantly higher impact on their decision process than if I had said it myself.

PREDATOR POINT

To be deemed useful, your Key Items to Consider List must help the buyer(s) in their selection process.

When to Use It

The Key Items to Consider List is one of the last things that you present to the inner circle in your initial meeting with them. It is always given to the committee as a "by the way" item as you are wrapping up the discussion. When providing a copy of this to each inner circle member, say

> As you go through your decision process, here is a list of criteria that are relevant to selecting vendors within my industry; I would recommend that you cover each of these points when you evaluate your different options. These will help you to make the best selection for your company's needs.

To summarize, eliminating competitors is achieved with your ability to differentiate yourself from all other options. Another key opportunity for differentiation lies in how you build and present your recommendations. I will cover this topic in detail in Chapter 8.

Chapter | 8

FORGET THE BUDGET

How to Present the Winning Proposal

Chapter 6 provided an action plan that included a meeting with the influencer and a second meeting with the inner circle, followed by a third and final meeting with everyone to present your proposal. Chapter 7 provided strategies for eliminating the competition from consideration. At this point in the selling cycle, we have conducted both needs analysis meetings, so the time now has come to prepare and present our recommendations to the inner circle. This chapter outlines an effective structure for both preparing your proposal and delivering an outstanding presentation. But first, let's take a look at whether or not you should adhere to the budget in preparing your proposal.

What a Budget Is—and Isn't

As we discussed in Chapter 4, in most competitive sales, a budget has already been established for the inner circle by the time that you and your competitors are contacted. With the budget in place, one of the most common mistakes that salespeople make is to first inquire what the budget is and then to build their proposal around the budget number. They automatically assume that the budget represents the maximum amount that the company is willing to spend to get what it needs. This is simply not true, and competitors who build their recommendations exclusively around the budget are doing a disservice to both themselves and the buyer.

Dominant predators do not sell to the budget; they sell to what they deem appropriate to the situation. They build solutions around the needs of the client first and then determine whether or not the recommendations they have prepared happen to fall under the budget limits set by the buyers. If this is the case, so much the better. If not, the situation is not viewed as an obstacle. They simply adjust their selling strategy, as we will discuss shortly.

PREDATOR POINT

Most competitors will sell to the budget. The dominant predator ignores it.

In the competitive sale, recognize any budget for what it is: a preliminary purchase estimate that is submitted by the inner circle and approved by the decision maker. The group makes its best guess as to what it will need to spend to acquire the desired outcome, usually "pads" it a bit to allow for unforeseen expenses, and submits it for approval. Once the budget is approved, the inner circle is expected to stay within those guidelines. However, in no way does this mean that the group is prevented from getting additional funding if it cannot get what it wants within the original budget—or if its perceived needs change during the course of making the decision.

A simple example of this process is the way most of us purchase a new automobile. We do our research (in most cases online), and then we go to the dealership with our "budget" set, thinking that we know both exactly what we are going to buy and what we are going to spend. At the dealership, this initial position often changes. We discuss our known needs and spending limit with a skilled salesperson, who makes us aware of options and other available add-ons for the model that we had not considered or did not fully understand in terms of buyer benefit. We might not have realized, for example, just how pleasant a heated driver's seat would be in the dead of winter until our salesperson activated this feature during the test drive. Or, in my case, I never considered adding the rear-view camera option in my last new vehicle until the salesperson showed me how much easier backing up to my boat trailer would be when using this feature. Once these additional options are introduced into the decision process, our original purchase plan—and spending limit—has changed. We have new needs that we had not identified previously, and in many cases we end up investing more than the initial budget to satisfy those needs.

The process that your inner circle uses to make its buying decision is no different. Keep in mind here that the inner circle budget was based on "known"—public information—needs. These were the initially identified issues that prompted the opportunity but do not include any private information areas that you uncovered with your secondary needs analysis questions. The only real issue here—and the one that dominant predators seize on—is whether or not the best solution for the full spectrum of customer needs—public and private—can be obtained within the budgetary boundaries. If the client wants something that will exceed the budget—a result, in most cases, of your private information needs analysis—he or she almost always will ask for, and receive, the additional money to obtain it.

This does not mean that you should try to sell a solution that exceeds the budget. It simply means that you should take into account that the ideal solution may or may not fall within the budget guidelines. You should therefore be prepared to set aside the budget number in order to deliver the ideal solution for the client.

PREDATOR POINT

Dominant predators use private information topics to make the budget inadequate for the needs of the client.

Don't assume, however, that the prospective client is going to simply treat the budget as a nonissue in the buying decision. The company has established a maximum expenditure number for the purchase, and we are obligated to respect, and address, that number. However, we are by no means limited to selling to it.

The Two-Choice Approach to Dealing with Budgets

Once you have established the budget of the client, prepare two different and completely separate proposals. The first proposal—the one that the inner circle has asked for and is expecting—outlines what you are prepared to do for them under the established budget constraints. Because the budget was formulated on internally identified needs, in most cases your "at budget" recommendation here will address only those issues which were public information in nature. This is the option in which the recommendations that you make will be similar logically to what your competitors submit.

Unlike your competitors, however, you are also going to provide what you consider to be the optimal solution—in other words, the best possible way to address the stated needs, both public and private, of the prospective buyers. In this second proposal, you will temporarily set the issue of money aside and first build the solution for the needs of the inner circle and then determine its associated cost.

Does this strategy actually work? Can you really eliminate your competition by ignoring budget constraints when everyone else sells to them? To answer this question, consider the following experience that I had with this approach—in this case as the buyer.

The Two-Choice Approach in Action

We had made a decision to change our company's Web site vendor because our company had outgrown the services of the firm that we had been working with. I set up a meeting with two competing firms to discuss our company's needs. I gave both the vendors involved a preliminary budget number during the respective initial meetings. I had no idea what my costs would be to accomplish what we wanted—a point worth noting because this is a common buyer position in the early stages of a competitive sale—but I knew what I would "like" to spend, so I gave both of them this low-ball number as a starting point. One of the firms met with me, discussed my needs, and came back in short order with a proposal that met my stated budget but also lacked much of what we wanted to accomplish. In fact, the firm attempted to address most of my stated needs within the budget by offering minimal and mostly inadequate solutions across the board.

The second firm took a different approach. This was a local Web hosting and development company; my first meeting was with the firm's CEO and two members of his staff. This "techie" was a first-rate sales person. His initial question to me was simple and straightforward:

"What do you want to accomplish?" This one topic-opening question took me nearly an hour to answer. During that initial discussion, he asked me numerous directive questions regarding specific expectations and desired outcomes. We had a very productive and in-depth conversation regarding the vision I had for my business as it related to the Internet.

At the end of the meeting, he concluded with this: "We will prepare two proposals for you. The first will be based on your budget and will show you what we can do for you for what you want to invest." This, of course, was exactly what his competitor also had done. "My second proposal," he continued, "will provide a complete overview of how we will accomplish everything that you want, including time frames and steps, but this second option will not apply to the budget figure that you gave to us."

This sounded reasonable, and as you would expect, I agreed to this plan of action. We met for the second time a week later, and he presented his two proposals to me in this fashion:

"First, let me show you what we can do for you based on what you want to spend." This initial presentation was brief, limited in scope, and quickly made it crystal clear to me that we could not get what we needed at my stated "budget" number.

"Now," he continued, setting that proposal aside, "let me show you what we recommend you do to take you where you want to go." During this second, much longer review, he went over, in great detail, how his firm would address all my stated needs, what the time frame would be for each one, what order he recommended we accomplish them in, and finally, what the cost would be for each item.

You should know that the investment required for the second option was, as you would expect, several times that of the "budget" option.

Would you like to venture a guess as to which vendor I chose to work with—and which of that vendor's two proposal options I ended up choosing?

The answer, of course, is the one that gave me what we needed—which, in this case, was the one that disregarded the budget number.

PREDATOR POINT

Influencers buy what the budget allows them to buy. Decision-makers buy whatever they want.

Presentations versus Proposals

Even if your competitors have the opportunity to present to the inner circle, most of them, like most salespeople, do not recognize that there is a difference between making a presentation and handing out a proposal. When they open their presentation meeting by distributing copies of their proposal, they make a critical strategic error—they lose control of the meeting. They abdicate their role as the center of attention to the just-distributed document. They focus the inner circle's attention on the proposal when it should instead be focused on the salesperson.

If you want to completely derail your ability to present value and send the presentation meeting into a tailspin, begin it by handing out your proposal. Experienced salespeople already know how the next act unfolds: The financial person in the group immediately opens his or her copy, skips over all relevant content, finds your pricing, and begins asking questions about it. Others in the group will quickly chime in with their own questions and concerns. You will now be on the defensive. You have turned what was supposed to be a presentation into an exercise in haggling—and, worst of all, nobody in the group has any idea at this point about what they are getting for the investment. Does this sound like a good idea to you?

Dominant predators do not make this mistake. They do not present proposals; they present *themselves*. They manage the presentation meeting with one goal in mind—to demonstrate their understanding of the prospective account's needs and to showcase their expertise as a solution provider. They maintain control of events; they—and not the proposal—hold the spotlight, and the document is a support tool for the salesperson, not the other way around.

In a well-executed presentation meeting, the proposal therefore is simply a leave-behind, a hard-copy version of what is first covered in the actual presentation. It serves a singular purpose—to provide a record of what was covered by the presenter in the meeting. Beyond that, the skill of the salesperson carries the day—and wins the decision.

PREDATOR POINT

Handing out copies of your proposal at the start of the meeting surrenders your control of the meeting.

An important aspect of the proposal structure, though, is the choice of format. Because you are making a presentation, the worst thing that you can do when designing a proposal is to *write* it. The reason is simple: You cannot present text effectively to an audience. Nobody in your audience has the time to read your proposal, and nobody—at least, nobody who is controlling the decision—is going to read it. To hold the prospect's interest, your format for the proposal document must be logical, easy to follow, and quickly reviewable. For this reason, forego a text-based software program for creating proposals. Use a slide-presentation format, such as Microsoft PowerPoint, for your proposal pages. Design the overhead presentation first, and make the handout of this presentation your proposal document.

This makes the entire presentation/proposal process seamless and saves you valuable time. For the prospective account, it makes the postpresentation review a snap. By simplifying the amount of content in your document, you make it easy for the prospective account to recall virtually everything that you covered in your presentation.

Unlike your competitors, therefore, you will not begin your presentation by passing out documents to the attendees. Instead, you will present the proposal, one slide at a time, and speak to your audience, the proposal merely providing "talking points" as a backdrop for your communication skills. This very effective format places you in a leadership role throughout the meeting. It ensures that you maintain control, engage your audience, and sustain their undivided attention.

PREDATOR POINT

When presenting to one or two people, use your laptop. For groups of three or more, use an overhead projector and screen.

This strategy sets up a huge competitive advantage for you. Since the document that you have produced mirrors the presentation on the screen, there is no need for the audience to have a copy of your proposal during the presentation. This will be explained to the group as part of your agenda, as you will see shortly.

Three Steps for Structuring Your Proposal

As you have seen with the prior steps of the competitive selling process, dominant predators go into competitive sales with a battle plan, and they follow that plan. They take charge of each opportunity. They execute the steps outlined in this book, and they do not deviate significantly from one selling situation to another. Although certain variables may change, they do the same things, at the same time, every time. As is the case with any learned skill, the more they practice the process, the more successful they become at executing it.

This adherence to structure is especially important when executing the presentation meeting because, unlike the needs analysis, in this one you are doing most of the talking. By using an effective blueprint around which your recommendations are delivered, and by repeatedly following this structure in each opportunity, you, over time, continually improve your ability to be credible and persuasive. You come across as being well organized, polished, and professional—all attributes that enhance your chances of winning.

That said, the structure for delivering your formal presentation always begins with these three steps:

1. Overview of your company
2. Review of key client objectives
3. Presentation of solutions

Step 1: Opening the Presentation Meeting

As the person who asked for the presentation meeting, you have an obligation to explain your plan for using the group's time. Just as you did with the needs analysis, you will use an agenda to open this meeting. In this case, the structure for the proposal also doubles as the agenda for the presentation meeting:

INTRODUCTION

Thank you for this opportunity. I plan to present my recommendations to the group first, and I will then provide copies of my presentation to everyone at the end of the meeting. Here is how I would like to proceed:

PROCEDURE

First, I will provide a brief overview of my company—our history, our current market position, and our plans for the future.

I will then review in detail the key issues that we discussed from our previous meeting(s) to ensure that I have a thorough understanding of what you are looking for.

Next, I will present our recommendations, and I will show you why we have the best solution for your company's needs and objectives.

Following my presentation, I will review pricing, answer any final questions that you have, and if appropriate, discuss a next step.

CLOSE

How does this sound to everyone?

The "Nod Party"

Watch the inner circle carefully as you ask this last question. The question, "How does this sound to everyone?" is known as a *trial close question*—a question that asks for approval on a minor decision not related to the final one. Throughout the meeting, you will be looking for a positive response to any trial close questions that you ask of your Inner Circle. The reaction that you always want is a "nod party"—everyone nodding in agreement. You will use trial close questions throughout the presentation and closing process to "take the pulse" of the group and make sure that everyone is on board.

Whenever you ask a trial close question, look for the "nod party" response. This gives you the green light to move on to the next step in your process. If you get a concern or objection, welcome it—and deal with it immediately.

The Company Overview

Because you are competing against other options, it is especially important to begin your proposal with a brief summary of your company's strengths, market position, and philosophy. In a competitive selling environment, the inner circle members have a heightened interest in each vendor's "story"; information about each of your respective companies helps them in their overall decision process. The best company overviews are *brief* and, most important, *interesting*. *Brief* means that you should limit this portion of the meeting to three or four minutes; after all, this meeting is primarily about them, not about you. *Interesting* means that your goal at this point is to grab and hold their attention. Therefore, strive to tell a good story:

- Explain how your company got its start. Talk about your founders and how the business began.
- Review the key events in the history of the business, where the company is today, and your company's plans for the future.
- Wherever possible, tie in aspects of your company's strengths with items of importance to your prospects. For example, the fact that your firm has a staff of 16 system-trained technicians to support the client base is merely a statistic, but if having knowledgeable technical support is an important issue to your prospective account, then this would be an appropriate aspect of your company overview to mention at this time.

After the brief but interesting company overview, the time comes to delve into the issues that brought you and the buyers together in the first place.

Step 2: Review of Key Client Objectives

Most salespeople assume that presenting recommendations effectively is the key step in the presentation meeting. In a competitive selling situation, this is simply not true; in fact, the recommendation step here is almost an afterthought. It is the review of client objectives that makes or breaks each competitor during the presentation phase of the process. This is because the review of client objectives is the culmination of the time and effort that you have invested to this point. It is your one opportunity to demonstrate to the inner circle that you more than any other competitor have a clear and complete grasp of the issues that motivated them to call each of you in the first place. Remember, the inner circle wants to work with an *advisor*—someone who has the depth of knowledge and understanding to deliver real value. Simply stated, if you do a superb job with this portion of the meeting, you will leave your competitors in your wake.

We now come to a point in the selling cycle where your earlier ability to gain an interview with the inner circle pays off. Remember that your competitors' source for client needs was limited to public information needs provided by the influencer. Their list of client issues therefore will be limited to information from that one source. This is the point in the process at which they are the most vulnerable—and you now have the opportunity to deliver a knockout blow.

Success Lies in the Details

During the review of client objectives, your competitors will compound the limitation of having only public information by simply listing off those issues. In terms of communicating value, this is both inadequate and ineffective. Keep in mind that this is the point at which you demonstrate your level of understanding regarding the issues that your prospects want to address. Their vendor selection therefore will be heavily influenced by which competitor "gets it"— in other words, which resource truly understands what they are trying to accomplish. Depth is therefore paramount when executing the review of client objectives. You must be thorough and spare no details. Completely review, one at a time, the specific points for each area of need. This means that for each issue identified, you

- State what need is created by the issue
- Review how it is affecting the prospect's business and to what extent
- Review the current status of the issue
- Review the desired prospect objective regarding that issue

What does this look like in practice? To demonstrate the difference between glossing over client issues and effectively reviewing them, I will use a simple example: Assume that two competing companies provide janitorial cleaning services to businesses. The potential client, a bank, is changing vendors because its annual contract is up for renewal. The buyers are considering two new janitorial vendors for the cleaning needs of the business; I will call the two competing sales-people the "competitor" and the " predator."

Both the competitor and the predator met with the influencer, and the following three issues were communicated as public infor-mation needs by the influencer and outlined in the request for proposal (RFP):

- The chosen vendor must meet the bank's expectations for cleanliness.

- The chosen vendor must provide trained, conscientious employees.
- The chosen vendor must be able to provide service on Thursday and Sunday evenings.

Unlike the competitor, the predator requested and was granted a meeting with the inner circle group. In this second discussion, the predator also learned from those present at the inner circle meeting that the bank the following information:

1. There had significant language-barrier issues between the facilities manager, who is responsible for the cleanliness of the bank, and the prior janitorial service's employees.
2. The client had significant problems with the quality of work of the previous cleaning service in cleaning the carpet, particularly in areas of high foot traffic.
3. The bank had grown frustrated with the amount of turnover among the prior service's cleaning staff.

Now both the competitor and the predator are in the process of reviewing client needs at their respective presentation meetings. Here is how the competitor reviews his understanding of the cleaning needs of the bank:

First, you want a janitorial service that will meet your standards for cleanliness. Second, your selected vendor must provide employees who are properly trained. Third, you want your cleaning performed on Tuesday and Friday evenings.

Do you think that the competitor communicated a thorough understanding of the bank's cleaning needs? Here is the same step executed by the predator:

Based on our earlier meetings, here are the issues that I understand your bank wants to address with its next janitorial cleaning partner:

First, because you are a financial institution, presenting a clean, crisp image to your customers is a top priority. This is especially important in the lobby area, which gives customers their first impression of your facility and is also the site of most building traffic. So a priority for your cleaning needs is to partner with a service that will address all of your specific requirements and place a premium on ensuring that your lobby area is thoroughly cleaned and reflects well on the business to all visitors.

Next, you have had a poor experience with the quality of work that your prior service performed, and you feel that this is primarily due to an inability of that vendor to train and retain quality employees. Because of their turnover problem, you have had to repeatedly get involved with the prior vendor's staff to ensure that each new employee understood your expectations. This was redundant and time-consuming for you. So a stable, well-trained workforce will be a requirement of whatever vendor you select.

You also stated that because you experience your highest volume of customer traffic on Fridays and Saturday mornings, you must have your cleaning performed on Thursdays and Friday evenings. You have found in the past that planning your cleaning program around your peak traffic times ensures that the facility looks its best during the entire week. So any vendor that you select will need to adhere to this schedule. You also expect that the work will be performed between the hours of 8 and 11 p.m. and will not exceed three hours per visit.

Additionally, I understood that there was a significant and consistent language barrier between your office management and members of the prior vendor's cleaning crews; many of their staff did not have an adequate grasp of English, and this resulted in difficulty in both communicating expectations and correcting discrepancies. In a number of cases, your office manager was required to use a subordinate at the bank to act as an interpreter for members of the cleaning crew, which interfered with this staff member's duties at the bank on a regular basis. So, with your new service, a thorough grasp of English will be required of all cleaning staff members.

Next, a continual problem in the past has been the carpet in your lobby area, especially the area between the front door and the teller windows. Because this is the highest traffic area in the bank, it requires an extra level of care and effort to prevent a visible path from shoe traffic. Your prior service did not meet your expectations here, and you have had customers comment negatively on the look of this area. You require that your next vendor pay special attention to cleaning the carpet and to permanently eliminate this problem.

Finally, your prior service had continual problems with employee turnover. This resulted in the regular presence of cleaning staff who were not familiar with your cleaning procedures and continually made mistakes. Your facilities manager had to regularly work with these new employees to ensure that they understood the bank's expectations, which was very time-consuming and contributed to your overall dissatisfaction with the quality of work performed. So any new vendor that you work with must be able to demonstrate a track record of employee retention to your bank in order to win your business.

Notice a "slight" difference between the competitor and the dominant predator during the execution of this step? Now you see why, if this part of the presentation is executed properly, you are likely to be anointed the vendor of choice before the actual presentation of recommendations ever takes place.

Summarizing the Review

At the end of the review of client objectives, you must take care to ensure that you have three key points in your favor:

- You have correctly addressed any and all the issues of the potential client.
- There are no other outstanding issues that need attention.
- Everyone is on board with the items just reviewed.

To ensure that this is the case, ask these two questions at the end of the review of client objectives:

1. *"What other issues does the group have that I have not addressed?"* Wait for a response. If there are any "surprises" here, deal with them. Usually, there will be none—you will encounter silence. This is exactly the reaction that you want. Then ask the same question in a different way:
2. *"Have I addressed everyone's issues?"* Another trial close question—therefore, look for the "nod party." And—as covered in Chapter 5—be on the lookout for the sniper.

Step 3: Presentation of Solutions

In a competitive sale, the winning proposal will be the set of solutions that provides the best possible fit for the prospective buyer's objectives. Salespeople often forget this point when putting together recommendations. They think that the competitor who includes the most "stuff" in his or her proposal has, through sheer volume of information, an advantage over the other vendors. Preoccupied with what their competitors are proposing, they can't resist the temptation to make the account aware of some irrelevant capability or new technology, and they insert this, uninvited, into the proposal. This is done irrespective of the fact that such items were never discussed during the earlier meetings, nor did the prospective buyers express any interest in seeing them.

The Principle of Matching

When putting together a competitive proposal, remember that anything you include that does not relate directly to a stated need of the buyer serves no positive purpose. In fact, including such add-ons only serves to water down the impact of your recommendations, confuse the buyer, and waste his or her time. Therefore, the ideal proposal is one that provides a perfect fit between the needs of the client and the capabilities of the seller:

Stated need → Solution
Stated need → Solution
Stated need → Solution

This means that this portion of your proposal is clear, succinct, and to the point. Each recommendation mirrors a specific stated need of your buyer. The message communicated to the buyer is also simple: You listened to them, you understand their issues, and you are prepared to provide an optimal level of value. Let your competitors muddy the water with add-ons and irrelevant data. When competing for business, clarity is key.

This is the point at which the inner circle will want to know, "What is this going to cost?" This question begins the negotiation process, which I will cover in Chapter 9.

Chapter | 9

GAINING THE UPPER HAND

Negotiation in the Competitive Sale

At the end of the presentation, the next logical step in the process is the review of fees. Keep in mind that because you are making your presentation before handing out the proposal, there has been no opportunity here for a "sneak preview" of your pricing. This detail is important; controlling the flow of information allows you to segue from the presentation of solutions to the subject of money. This ensures that when you present your pricing, the group is seeing this information for the first time.

Following the presentation of fees, the inner circle likely will want to negotiate on your pricing. Chapter 10 will provide detailed steps regarding how to present fees properly, handle price objections, and ask for the business. However, before we delve into the skills involved in closing, we need to have a thorough understanding of negotiation as it relates to the competitive sale.

Common Assumptions About Negotiation

When it comes to negotiating fees, there are two assumptions that many salespeople make out of habit, and in most cases they are totally incorrect. The first assumption is that in a competitive sale the issue of price is the determining factor in vendor selection. This is the mind-set of the order-taker salesperson, and it assumes that all options being presented are fundamentally the same. It is also completely out of place in this selling environment. Keep in mind the point made in Chapter 1—that if the buyer has the financial ability to pay for your offering, price is eliminated as a reason for losing to a competitor. Remember, also, that this is a competitive sales opportunity—you and the other vendors were called in to discuss a preestablished need. Hence there is no need here to persuade your buyers to spend money; the funds have already been budgeted. So the issue here is not whether or not the buyer has the funds to make a decision but rather which competitor is going to receive those already-allocated funds. This decision will be based on which option presents the best solution for the preapproved investment and therefore has little to do with the issue of cost.

The second assumption that most salespeople make here is that the buyer, and not the salesperson, holds the upper hand during the negotiation process. In other words, the salesperson assumes that his or her desire to sell to the buyer exceeds the buyer's interest in doing business with the salesperson. This causes the salesperson to mentally assume a position of weakness—and an irrational willingness to drop the initially proposed price to win the business.

Dominant predators negotiate from a position of strength. They recognize that dropping their price without a corresponding drop in value is not negotiating; it's quitting. It is the default position for those who do not know how to manage the sales process, do not differentiate themselves from their competition, and take a "me too" approach to the competitive sale. It is also an admission that you lack the confidence to stand your ground, that you do not believe in the value of your product or service, and that you refuse to ask to be paid what you are worth.

This last point hits you right in the pocketbook. If you are a commissioned salesperson, a reduction in your price also will result in a corresponding reduction in your income. This means that a fee-reduction request is no different from a request for you to accept less compensation than you have earned for the work that you have performed. You have worked hard to earn this client's business. Why should you not be paid what you are worth? Why should you accept a cut in pay to make a sale?

> ## PREDATOR POINT
>
> Learning to negotiate properly has the same effect as giving yourself a raise.

Dominant predators don't accept substandard compensation because they don't make substandard sales. Their position—always—is that an initial price is never reduced without a corresponding drop in products or services provided. This means that they won't cut their price to get business. The good news is that, in most cases, they don't have to.

The Opening Position of the Buyer

Once all competitive proposals have been submitted, the inner circle will first—without regard to quoted fees—select the competitor with whom they want to do business. This is the second *tier* of the selection process, and it is when the choice of vendor is made. Then, and only then, will they bring up the issue of negotiating—and this step tells you volumes about where you stand in their decision process.

Conventional wisdom in selling would have you believe that receiving a price objection from a buyer here is a negative event. In reality, it is just the opposite. It is one of the strongest indications a buyer can make that he or she wants to do business with you, and I can prove it with the following example.

Several years ago, I was in the market for a copier. I looked at several models from several vendors—I will refer to these as Competitors A, B, and C. All three of the models that I was considering had similar features, similar capabilities, and similar pricing. At the end of my assessment, it was clear to me that Competitor C was the best choice of the three options I was considering.

At this point, I went back to one of the three options, and only one, and to that one I said, "Your price is too high."

Which of the three was it, and why?

The answer, of course, is Competitor C—the one that I had decided I *wanted to do business with.*

Why did I not also give a price objection to Competitors A and B?

Because I had no desire to do business with them, *which made the issue of negotiating irrelevant in both cases.*

PREDATOR POINT

A request to negotiate lets you know that you are the vendor of choice.

So you see, when a buyer approaches you with a desire to negotiate, he or she is not causing problems for you. Instead, the buyer is making a very clear and positive statement that he or she wants to do business with you. In fact, a price objection from your buyers is the single most clear indicator, prior to an actual announcement, that you have been selected as the vendor of choice.

So the buyer's desire to negotiate with you tells you that you have been picked—and that you are no longer, in most cases, competing with other options. This is obviously great news—and something you probably have never stopped to consider. Does this mean that you should respond to this positive development with a willingness to immediately drop your fees? Hardly.

The Opening Position of the Dominant Predator

Dominant predators know that they hold the upper hand as the negotiating process begins. This is so because they have followed the process outlined in this book, and they therefore recognize that the following points are in their favor:

- They have provided overwhelming evidence, in the form of biography sheets, references, and letters of recommendation, that they deliver outstanding results for their clients. They have thus positioned themselves as the least risky option to the inner circle because their ability to demonstrate value exceeds, by a wide margin, anything submitted by their competitors. No other options will get any further serious consideration.
- They have, through the use of two needs analysis meetings, identified both public and private information needs with the influencer and the inner circle. They have therefore broadened both the scope of the client's needs and the spectrum of value that they are capable of providing. The other competitors will

be limited to serving public information needs, and the perception of the buyers will be that they do not match the dominant predator's ability to deliver value.

- They have given highly effective visual presentations, supported by proposals that match up with the client's desired outcomes in a way that exceeds anything that the other vendors have produced.
- They have presented two appropriate options as choices for the buyer—one that meets the client's stated budget and provides the maximum allowable value for what the client is willing to spend and one that provides the optimal solution for the client's stated needs but ignores the budget.

Thus, when the inner circle asks the dominant predator to negotiate, they are unknowingly confirming that they have made their vendor selection decision. The dominant predator recognizes that he or she has successfully changed the decision dynamic. *The choice to be made is no longer whether the dominant predator is the selected vendor, but rather which of the two options that the dominant predator presented will be used.* The conversation among the inner circle at this point is no longer, "Who do we want to do business with?" but rather "Can we get what we need from [the dominant predator] within our original budget, or are we willing to spend more to get the optimal solution that [the dominant predator] recommends?"

PREDATOR POINT

When negotiations begin, the decision is no longer "who?" but rather "what?"

Although they may have yet to be informed, your competition is not normally a factor at this point. In most cases, you are no longer competing for the business; you are now competing to maintain your fees and corresponding margins irrespective of what the final option for purchase becomes.

Three Negotiation Tactics the Inner Circle Will Use Against You

Once the vendor-selection decision is made, the inner circle will approach you with the request to negotiate your initial recommendations. Negotiating is a standard part of the purchase process, and you must be prepared to work through the steps with your buyers. Three of the most common ways that buyers do so are outlined below, with a corresponding strategy for dealing with each of them.

Tactic 1: The Freebie Request

In this scenario, the initial negotiation tactic is of the something-for-nothing variety; the buyer will attempt to get you to add "freebies" as a condition of purchase. In most cases, this will involve blending your two proposals. They will want you to include resources from the optimal-solution proposal as a part of the at-budget proposal—at no additional cost, of course.

To formulate your response, you should first consider the position of the buyers as they make this request. The most common reason that you are being asked to do this is because the inner circle sees value in your optimal-solution recommendations but does not want to have to ask for more money to get them. This is understandable, but since it is something that they would just rather avoid if they can do so, it is therefore not enough of an issue to make it a deal breaker. The fact is that the step needed here—to have them ask for more money than initially budgeted for the purchase—is nothing more than a minor inconvenience to the group. Furthermore, the worst outcome possible in making that request would be that it is declined, in which case the inner circle simply would be back to its original negotiating position with you.

Thus there is nothing to stop your buyers from looking for additional funds—but they have no reason to do so if you are willing to give them what they want for free. If you make it clear that you are not willing, they are very likely to request the extra funding. Your initial reaction to this request therefore must be strong. You must hold your ground. There is value in the additional items requested, and you have every right to expect compensation for that value. Before discussing any adjustments to your initial proposals, a determination needs to be made regarding whether or not funds are available to pay for the additional items. The inner circle does not, in most cases, have direct authority to determine this monetary matter. They therefore need their ranking member to go "upstairs" to the original decision maker on what amounts to a fund-raising expedition. If they want what you recommended badly enough, you can motivate your buyers to take this step.

How to Handle the "Freebie" Request

If you were to cooperate with this request—to provide items to this client at no charge when you require payment for them from any other client—you would be, in effect, overcharging everyone else. How do you think your other clients would react if they found out that they were paying for something that this client was receiving for free?

The appropriate way to handle this situation, then, is to explain this point to the inner circle and, as the leader in the sales process, to recommend a next step. As follows:

Our policy on this issue is that we maintain price integrity when it comes to our fee structure because it would not be fair to our other clients to provide free services to you that are paid for by them. So, for that reason, I cannot include these other items without charging for them.

My suggestion would be that you determine internally if these additional items warrant the additional investment, and then we can determine how to best proceed. How does that sound?

This strategy puts the ball back in the inner circle's court. If the items that were requested are important in terms of value, the inner circle will agree with this suggestion—and, in most cases, will come back to you in short order with a "new" budget that allows for these items. And if they don't get that new budget, there is no harm done— you simply revert to the original negotiating position.

PREDATOR POINT

If the inner circle agrees with your suggestion, offer to participate in the meeting with the decision maker.

Some of you who read this book will reflect on this point and think that you are missing an opportunity to close the sale. "If you would just bow to their demands, you could walk out with the order right now!" they will say. This may be—but what's the hurry? Good salespeople know when to be patient, and this is one of those occasions that calls for it. Let's not forget that the decision is no longer which competitor will get the business—you have been selected, and that decision is done. The issue at hand is no longer yes or no but only *what*. Give the inner circle an opportunity to work within the parameters that you set, and you will learn in short order whether or not the additional items in your optimal proposal are of sufficient value to the client to warrant paying for them. This strategy demonstrates that you are willing to work with the group to meet their needs, and they will respect you for maintaining your fee integrity.

Tactic 2: The Carrot Trick

A second tactic the inner circle will use after choosing a vendor is to inform the chosen competitor that he or she has been selected—the dangling of the proverbial carrot—and then leverage this announcement by attempting to make the awarding of the business contingent on a reduction of the winner's fees.

I ran into the carrot trick during a competitive decision process for a speaking engagement. The client was putting together a national sales meeting, and I was one of several speakers being considered. The decision committee was headed by the CFO, who in this case controlled the budget. We had a good initial discussion, and in short order I provided my recommendations to the group. Following my proposal submission, the CFO called me and asked for a follow-up meeting to review my program recommendations. At this meeting, which included only the two of us, he began with some good news: "We would like for you to be our speaker at our upcoming conference." (There's that carrot!) "However"—he paused for effect—"we are already over budget for the meeting—airfare expenses and hotels have used up most of our allocated funds—so I am faced with the problem of finding ways to reduce our costs. Therefore, I was wondering . . . would it be possible for you to help me out here with your speaking fee?"

Handling the Carrot Trick

As with the "freebie" request, the carrot trick is, at the core, a request to commit a violation of ethics. The client doesn't see it that way, of course, so it becomes necessary here to tactfully explain this point. In my case, the client was asking me to perform work for a fee that was lower than what other clients pay me. This is not fair to my other clients. So the only appropriate response to the request was what I said—and what you should say—when faced with the dangling carrot:

> My policy on this issue is that I consider it unethical to charge two different clients two different fees for the same amount of value. So, for that reason, I regret that I cannot do that. I will guarantee your satisfaction with the quality of my work and that you will receive the full value of your investment.

I fully expected his reaction to be "See you later" and was fully prepared for this outcome. Instead, he said, "I see your point" and hired me at my stated fee. Best of all, I worked with his company as a speaker on two subsequent occasions, and in neither case did we ever have another conversation about my fees.

It is worth taking a moment to consider the ramifications of what would have happened had I agreed to the lower initial fee. If I had, every subsequent engagement that I had with this client would have been subject to the same negotiation exercise, now made redundant because nothing that I quoted in terms of my fee would be taken seriously initially. For me, this agreement would have resulted in a one-way street of wasted time and lost income. This is why salespeople who follow such a policy of discount on request are doomed to be overworked and underpaid; they not only lose money each time they engage in such practices, but they also have to endure the drain on their selling time that this process requires to get the discounted sale closed.

Tactic 3: The Match Game

The third and most common postselection negotiating tactic involves making your official selection contingent on your willingness to meet price points quoted by your competition—an attempt to commoditize your recommendations by providing your products or services for the same fees that an inferior provider has quoted. "We are interested in doing business with you—but will you match your competitor's price?" is the usual request.

This tactic, a favorite among purchasing managers, is nothing but a fishing expedition. You already know that the buyer would not have raised the subject of doing business with you unless you were the vendor of choice. The only thing attractive about your competitor's offering is that the price associated with it is lower than yours—and that's hardly a reason to match it.

More important, your value proposition is not the same as that of your competition. You have removed the issue of comparing apples to apples from the buying decision, so the buyers cannot get what you offer from anyone else—and they know it. Why, then, would you think it feasible to "match" someone else's inferior recommendation? The truth is that they don't think it is either—they simply want to see what your reaction will be. If your reaction is to drop your price, so much the better—you just unnecessarily gave away your margins without a basis for doing so.

Handling the Match Game

As with the other two scenarios, in this case your opening position is to hold your price position. Remind the buying group that you provide a premium level of service and quality, as demonstrated both in your proof-of-performance documentation and your proposal. Refer again to the issue of price integrity—that you deviate from your pricing structure because this would not be fair to your other clients. In short, politely tell them that you are not in business to be the least expensive option. Rest assured, they will understand—and they will respect you for sticking to your guns. If they insist on this point, there is a way to work within their parameters, and you will learn it in Chapter 10.

The Buyer's Bluff

You have surely noticed by now that in each negotiating scenario that I have presented, your default position is always the same—to hold the line on your price. It may appear that you are unwilling to work with the client to find an acceptable compromise; nothing could be further from the truth! Don't assume that these tactics mean that you have no room to negotiate—you have plenty of room, and I will cover how to use it in Chapter 10. You need to recognize, however, that there is a world of difference between finding a mutually agreeable solution—one that provides the client with what they need while protecting your margins—and simply cutting your rates on request.

For now, know that the reason for maintaining your fee structure is that the buyer's bluff is in effect in most of these negotiating strategies. The *buyer's bluff* is a term used to describe any attempt by the inner circle to make you think that you must reduce your fees to earn their business. Don't believe it! In most cases you will find that this is not the case. If you are selling value properly, most attempts at price negotiation are nothing more than a half-hearted attempt to save a few bucks. There is rarely a logical rationale for requesting the reduction; the buyers simply want to see what they can get on request. They have the right to do this, but you also have the right to say "No."

If you have followed the steps outlined in this book, the buyers will be well aware of the fact that no other option considered can approach your ability to provide value. This knowledge puts them in a tough position: Either pay a fair price for your recommendations or be satisfied with an inferior alternative. Be confident that your buyers will make the right decision—after all, in most cases they had no reason to request a lower price in the first place.

> ## PREDATOR POINT
>
> The initial negotiation position of the dominant predator is always to stand firm on their initial pricing.

The Real Cost of Haggling

Most buyers consider it a victory when they persuade a salesperson, through these various haggling methods, to cut the price to get the buyer's business. The harsh reality is that most of the time the old adage "You get what you pay for" holds true in short order for this type of business relationship. Allow me to explain why.

All businesses, including yours, have limited resources available for sale to their customer base. Whether you sell products or services, there is a limit to the number of customers that you can adequately service at one time. If you are in a product-based business, your inventory is your limitation. If you sell cable advertising, air-time spots during prime-time viewing is your limitation. If you have a consulting practice, the number of people whom you can allocate to any one project is your limitation. In any business that sells, resources are finite.

In any situation where the demand for resources exceeds the available supply, someone is going to get what they need, and someone is going to go without. Choices have to be made by the vendor regarding which clients get those resources. Assume, then, that you have two clients; one of them pays the full asking price for an item that you carry, and one pays a lower, discounted price. If both these clients want something that you have, and you only have enough of it to satisfy the needs of one, you know full well which client is going to get the needed item. The answer, of course, is the one that is paying you the full value of those goods and services. The client left out in the cold—the one being inconvenienced—is the one that got you to discount your fees. So an earlier victory for them now has become a major liability.

The point here is that when you discount your fees, both parties pay a price. You, as the seller, are paid less than what you deserve, and they, as the customer, inevitably get the short end of the stick when it comes to allocating available resources. This principle applies to everything—customer service, technical support, etc. Priorities are determined by profitability—and the less profitable the client, the lower that client falls in the resource-allocation pecking order.

This exact scenario played out in my business some years ago. I dropped my fees to win business on this occasion, and it was a decision that both the client and I lived to regret. This particular company was represented by a vice president who was also a world-class haggler. In this case, the business was within a short driving distance of my office. I had proposed a customized training program for the company's sales force, with the initial training program to be followed up with four quarterly reinforcement sessions. When I presented my fees, my haggler repeatedly attempted to persuade me to drop them for the initial training program. When I made it clear that I was not willing to do so, he abandoned this strategy. In true haggler fashion, he then tried a different tact; he began asking for a discount on the quarterly reinforcement sessions. Because this was a client that would not require any air travel to work with, and because I had also momentarily lost control of my faculties, in a moment of poor judgment I agreed to this request. Yes, I admit it—I agreed to do the quarterly reinforcement sessions for a lower fee than my other clients paid me.

The training program, when it was delivered, was a big success; the client was very pleased with the deliverable.

Then the time came for phase two—the quarterly reinforcement sessions. I am ashamed to admit this, but when the time arrived for these to take place, I found myself avoiding calling this client to schedule them. Conducting those sessions was not something that I wanted to avoid because of the work involved; I liked the company and enjoyed working with its people. The issue here was purely an economic one. You see, I had a full calendar of other clients who were willing to pay me my full fee, and this client, as you have seen, was not. Therefore, I found myself moving this client to the bottom of my priority list in favor of other clients who had not pushed down my fees. Once again, the issue of discounted pricing had interfered with the allocation of limited resources.

Eventually, the client called me to schedule the training sessions—but with a twist. In place of our original agreement, my haggler wanted me to develop new material for those quarterly sessions—while maintaining the same negotiated price!

As you would imagine, I flatly refused this request. After several discussions regarding this latest gambit—all of which, I might add, resulted in no agreement reached—I got a call from the company's CEO.

"What is going on here?" he demanded to know.

I explained the situation exactly as I just described it and told him that I could not, and would not, create new content for the fees that we had negotiated initially.

In true decision-maker fashion, he then asked this question: "Would you please just create the new material that we need? We will pay you what you are supposed to be paid."

Now we were getting somewhere. I, of course, agreed immediately to those terms. Shortly thereafter, the haggler left the company; I have been doing business with that firm ever since—and always at my normal rate.

Folding versus Walking

Regardless of your skill level in negotiating, there are going to be times when you will be dealing with a haggler who presents you with an ultimatum: "Either give us what we want at the price we are willing to pay, or we will take our business elsewhere." This demand leaves you with two simple choices: Either agree to their terms or lose the business.

Arguments can be made for both choices; some salespeople will say that it depends on each situation and that each case is different. I strongly disagree. My argument is that you should *always* walk away, and I will give you my reason.

Have you ever closed a sale in which the client gave you just such an ultimatum? One in which every virtually every drop of profit was squeezed from the deal by the time you closed it? One in which you had to work hard—extra hard—for very little reward at the end?

Of course you have. Now think about what kind of client this account turned out to be. Do any of the following attributes apply to this hardball negotiator?

- Doesn't pay on time
- Doesn't cooperate
- Doesn't keep commitments
- Doesn't meet established deadlines
- Doesn't follow through as promised
- Drives your customer-service department crazy
- Lowers morale
- Constantly complains
- Acts rude, unreasonable, and overly demanding

I could go on and on, but the question you will end up asking yourself is always the same: "What was I thinking when I agreed to take on this client?"

Put another way, if you show me a potential client who does not want to pay you what you are worth, I will show you a potential client that you should avoid like the plague. My experience has consistently been that people who force you into a "fold or walk" decision are people you don't want to do business with. Walk away—quickly—and let them wrap themselves around your competitor's axle instead. Better them than you!

PREDATOR POINT

To tactfully walk away from a bad sale, say "It appears that we may not be a good fit for one another."

Fortunately, these kinds of clients are few and far between. For everyone else, there is a way to get to "Yes" without negotiating your rates or your margins, and you will learn how in Chapter 10.

Chapter | 10

THE ART OF CLOSING

Getting to "Yes" Without Lowering Your Fees

To most people not in sales, the stereotype of a *closer* is a salesperson who won't take no for an answer, a pushy individual who applies pressure to buyers to get them to do want the seller wants. Traditional, old-school sales training methods are largely to blame for having created this perception, proffering all manner of "secrets" to closing business while ignoring the issue of creating a desire to buy in the first place. It is important that we set traditional perceptions aside and examine the proper steps for closing the competitive sale.

What, Exactly, Is *Closing*?

Contrary to popular opinion, consummating a sale should be the easiest part of the process for both the seller *and* the buyer. In fact, a salesperson who must use high-pressure gimmicks and cheesy techniques to get a "Yes" in the competitive sale is one who lacks the fundamental ability to sell value. He or she then must resort to such tactics to compensate for the fact that he or she cannot persuade a buyer to act favorably based simply on the merit of that salesperson's recommendations.

Dominant predators do not waste their time or that of their buyers on high-pressure gimmicks and cheap tricks. The simple fact of the matter is that what you have (or have not) done up to this point in the process already has determined whether or not you are going to close the sale; the buyer either wants to do business with you or does not by the time you enter the closing process. There is little that you can say or do now that is going to change that outcome.

On the other hand, if you have properly executed the steps outlined in this book, you have already been identified as the clear vendor of choice. If this is the case, closing should be a mere formality; the act becomes nothing more than making it easy for a buyer who is ready to say "Yes" to do so. So much for all the closing techniques that salespeople are taught over the years to successfully acquire new business. They don't amount to much if you haven't sold the value of your proposal.

So, at this point in the process, the decision is no longer *who* but only *what* or *which one*. Acting now as the chosen business partner, your responsibility to the client is to help him or her to make a well-informed business decision between the two options that you have presented. Your objective, then, is to lead the buyer to the natural conclusion of this decision—choosing the right solution that meets his or her needs and financial considerations.

PREDATOR POINT

The best "technique" for closing a sale is one that makes it easy for your client to say "yes."

Three Steps for Closing

As noted in Chapter 8, there are three steps in the closing process. These are

- Presentation of pricing
- Addressing of final concerns
- Discussion on a next step

Each of these steps in the closing process is an independent action that requires its own unique skill set. I will now provide an in-depth look at how to execute each of these individual steps to perfection.

Presentation of Pricing

When reviewing fees, you will make two separate pricing presentations, one for each of the two options that you just presented, and in the same order. First, you will cover the costs associated with the at-budget proposal option so that the inner circle can see what their currently allocated funds will enable them to purchase. Introduce the at-budget proposal by saying, "First, I will review my recommendations based on the budget that you have provided."

If there are price concerns for the at-budget recommendation, it is important to ask the group to postpone addressing those concerns until after you have presented the pricing for your other proposal. Your intent here is to make the at-budget pricing—and any concerns regarding it—irrelevant, as you will soon see.

Next, you will present the second, optimal-solution proposal. To introduce this one, say, "I will now review the investment for the solution that I feel is the best fit for your needs." Remember that this is the option that sets the budget issue aside. Again, using the process outlined later in this chapter, you will review the pricing for this second option.

This will be the solution that provides the most value, and your sequencing of the two options allows you to make this, and not the at-budget proposal, the focus of the group's attention—and the basis for further discussion. In fact, your goal is to have the inner circle weigh their budgeted needs against the optimal-solution proposal, not the one that meets the budget. Therefore, this order of sequence in your price presentations is ideal because the optimal-solution option contains significantly more value and therefore will be of considerably more interest to the group. In most cases, this usually results in the inner circle discarding the at-budget proposal option once and for all.

PREDATOR POINT

Dominant predators intentionally make their optimal-solution proposal the focus of the inner circle, and therefore the basis for any negotiation.

Also, you will, of course, need to address any price concerns of the group at the conclusion of this review. If you are going to have to negotiate, you would prefer to have the higher-priced optimal-solution proposal be the basis for that discussion, don't you agree? This strategy usually accomplishes that objective.

How to Present Pricing Properly

As with price objections, most salespeople consider the review of fees to be a negative event—the bitter pill that must be swallowed by the customer as a condition of doing business. This certainly can be the case—if you allow it to be. If executed properly, however, the presentation of pricing is a superb opportunity for you to summarize the value of your recommendations—and minimize price concerns in the process. The key is to follow a procedure that serves to reinforce the value of your recommendations relative to the investment.

Figure 10.1, to be used when presenting the pricing for each of your two proposal options, demonstrates the proper sequence for presenting your fees.

Figure 10.1

The proper way to present pricing.

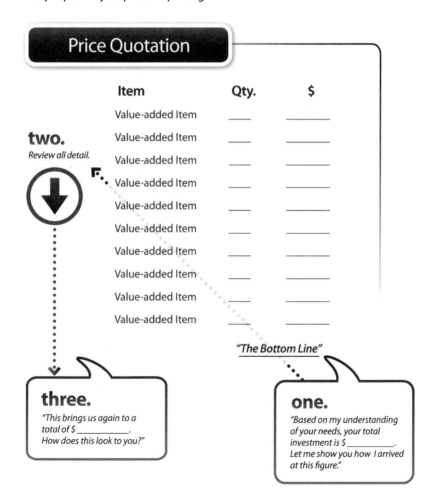

As noted in the figure, in each case, begin with the bottom-line total (one). You do this because the client will immediately focus on this number as soon as he or she sees the information being presented—and if you begin anywhere else, you will lose the client's attention. For this reason, you must start at the same place the client does. Point to the bottom-line total and say, as shown in the diagram, "Based on my understanding of your needs, your total investment for this option will be \$___. Let me show you how I arrived at this figure." Without hesitating, point to the first item in the upper left-hand corner—the top of your list referred to here as "Value-added Items"—and begin your review of each of these points (two), along with its respective portion of cost.

This strategy serves two purposes. The first is that it discourages a member of the inner circle from interrupting your momentum by injecting a price concern here. If an inner circle member has a concern about your fees, he or she certainly is entitled to it. He or she also will have an opportunity to bring that concern to your attention—just as soon as you have reviewed the full value the company is receiving for its investment, and not before.

The second purpose of this strategy is to shift the focus of the group away from the cost and back to the real issue of importance—what they are receiving for the investment. As you go through the list of items, take your time. Remind them of how each provides a solution to one of the needs from the Key Issues of Importance List. Your goal is to tilt the balance of value versus price in your favor.

The Price Review: Bundling versus Pricing Individual Items

The practice of *bundling* involves grouping multiple products or services together under one price so that the customer is not able to make yes-or-no decisions on individual price-line items. This allows the seller to piggyback add-ons and ancillary services without making each item's individual cost a factor in the overall buying decision.

In the competitive sale, bundling your pricing can cause you big headaches. For one thing, keep in mind that the buyers will have your competitor's pricing available for a point of comparison. If another vendor provides detailed, line-item pricing while you have bundled yours, this difference can make you appear to be devious or even dishonest to the buyers, an unnecessary hurdle to closing the sale. At the very least, you are likely to be put on the defensive and have to assign the individual price breakouts that you previously avoided so that the client will have a point of comparison. Another problem with bundling occurs during the negotiation process. If you quote a single price for multiple items and only have that one number to work with when handling a price objection, it makes the process of negotiating harder for you because you have less room in which to work.

While there are exceptions, avoid bundling your fees when you are competing for business. Clients like openness and honesty; the fact that you have nothing to hide will work in your favor. In addition, breaking out the detail of your fees works to your benefit in a big way when you are confronted with price objections, as you will see shortly.

When reviewing your pricing information for each proposal option, it is also critical that you include in the list anything that provides value to the client, *whether you charge for it or not*. In other words, if there are services that you do not typically charge for, such as design work, customer support, or free parts replacement, list these, and put the word *included* in the price field. Don't assume that the client takes these for granted. If you do not make it a point to list these value-added items, they will not be considered a part of your overall value proposition. Furthermore, it is possible that one of these included services or items may be perceived by someone in your audience to be the most value-added aspect of your proposal.

After completing this detailed review of pricing components, conclude your price presentation at (three) by saying, "This brings us again to a total investment of $_____."

Concluding the At-Budget Price Presentation

The only deviation made between presenting at-budget proposal pricing versus optimal-solution proposal pricing is here, at the very end of each presentation. When you have completed your review of the at-budget option, do not ask for feedback. Instead, maintain control of the presentation process by saying, "I will now review the pricing for my second proposal." This gives you the "bridge" you need to transition to the optimal-solution option and serves to shelve the at-budget option unless the group sees the need to revert back to it.

If one of the inner circle members has a concern or objection regarding the pricing of this proposal, do not make the mistake of interrupting your presentation flow to discuss the concern; instead, defer the question. "I would be happy to address questions regarding this proposal in a moment, but my preference would be to conclude the review of my second set of recommendations and then take any questions that you have. Would that be okay with the group?" Yes, it will be okay—so proceed. This allows you to maintain control and gets you to the second set of pricing—the set that will, in most cases, become the basis for the negotiation process.

Concluding the Optimal-Solution Price Presentation

Next, conduct a review of the optimal-solution proposal pricing in exactly the same sequence as you did with the at-budget one.

However, when concluding this second price review, ask the group for feedback, using a trial close question such as the one shown in (three) in the diagram: "How does this look to you?" You are now, for the first time, inviting a response from the group regarding your fees. Waiting until this point to make the request for input will engage their attention exclusively on the optimal-solution proposal pricing, causing the first one to be permanently discarded—which is exactly what you want.

At this point, as we transition from presenting fees to addressing final objections, it is important that you recognize the amount of control that you have exercised with regard to the flow of events. You presented two recommendations—one at budget and one that ignores the budget. You then presented associated fees for both proposals. By presenting the optimal-solution proposal last, you have focused the attention of the inner circle on the optimal-solution choice. In short, you will find that by following this process, you can expect few, if any, interruptions, and you will have led the buyers down a well-orchestrated and logical path that they want to follow with you.

Therefore, when you ask, "How does this look to you?" the response that you get will be one of the following three:

- "That looks good."
- "That's more than we want to spend."
- "We need to discuss this/think this over."

Addressing Final Concerns

Consider the level of confidence you will have when you know how to handle each of these three responses effectively. Let's take a look at how to do exactly that.

Handling the Positive Response

Any response to the question "How does this look to you" that is in the affirmative gives you the green light to ask for the order. Examples:

- "That looks good."
- "That will work."
- "That's about what we expected."
- "We like what we see."

When you receive this type of response, it is appropriate, of course, to ask for the business. I will cover how to do so in detail later in this chapter. However, when presenting two proposals—meaning that the best solution for the client exceeds the stated budget—this response is rare. Much more common are the other two—the price objection and the decision to postpone the decision. Let's take a detailed look at how to handle each of these situations, beginning with the one that you have the most problems with—price.

Handling "That's Too Much Money"

When the inner circle makes a statement such as "Your price is too high," they are initiating a discussion about money. The worst possible thing that you can do in this situation is to do what most salespeople do, which is to follow their lead. Examples include

- "Too much by how much?"
- "Where do I need to be?"
- "How far apart are we?"

The trap that salespeople fall into here—and it is a major negotiation error—is that when you respond to a question or statement about money with a question or statement of your own about money, you have "locked into" a price discussion—and have completely removed the issue of value from the table. To illustrate, consider the following exchange:

Buyers: "Your price is higher than your competition."
Salesperson: "How much higher?"

Do you see what has now happened? The ensuing conversation will be exclusively about the subject of money—and the question of value has been removed, permanently, from the discussion. There is a time to discuss the issue of money, but that time has not yet arrived. First, you need to change the subject.

PREDATOR POINT

Dominant predators never respond to a question or statement about money with a question or statement of their own about money.

Your Two Aces

If we liken the price-negotiation process to a game of poker, always remember that you begin the game by holding two aces. These cards take the form of the following assumptions:

1. That you have been selected as the vendor of choice
2. That the buyers do not feel your asking price is unreasonable relative to the value of what you are proposing

We have already established the validity of the first assumption; the buyers have concerns about your fees because they want to do business with you. The second assumption—that they do not feel your asking price is unreasonable to begin with—is worth taking a moment to consider.

When buyers tell you the "Your price is too high," they are not saying that you are overcharging for your products and/or services, nor are they saying that the amount of value in your proposal does not justify the investment. All they are saying is that there is a difference between what you are asking them to invest and what they are willing to spend. If you recognize this point for what it is, you will see immediately that there is no rational reason for you to simply cut the price of your proposed recommendations.

If these two conditions are in place—and they usually are—then you, and not the buyers, hold the upper hand in the negotiation process. Simply stated, your buyers want to buy from you as much as, if not more so than, you want to sell to them.

However, we still have the issue of the difference between the stated price and the desired one. There is a time to address this point—but it comes later, after you have established three key conditions relative to the buyer's negotiating position. You will establish these conditions by asking, in order, three critical questions.

Question 1: Is Your Recommendation Desired by the Buyer?

The first step in handling the price objection is to verify that the client actually wants to purchase what you have recommended. To confirm this, ask the following question, exactly as shown here: "If we set the fee issue aside for a moment, is the recommendation that I am making what you want?"

Note that the only answer that moves this conversation forward is, "Yes." If you do not get a positive answer to this first question, then you have nothing to negotiate. For example, if the response you get is, "We aren't sure yet," that's not a problem—but it does serve to take the issue of negotiating off the table until you (1) identify what they are not sure about and (2) address the issue. Your next question naturally would be what concerns they have exactly, after which you would, of course, address their answer.

Assuming that you do get a "Yes" to this question—and you usually will—you now will move to the second step in the process.

Question 2: Is the Price Objection Isolated?

You must next confirm that the fee involved is the only issue remaining on the table—in other words, that there are no other concerns besides the money involved. To do this, simply ask the question: "Is the price issue your only remaining concern at this point?"

Again, the only answer that moves this conversation forward is, "Yes." If there are any other issues—and there may be—the price issue is off the table, and you address the remaining concern. For example:

Salesperson: "Is the price issue your only remaining concern at this point?"
Buyers: "No, we are also concerned about whether or not your company can meet our technical support requirements."
Salesperson: "What concerns you about our ability to do this?"

Note here that the salesperson is now attempting to handle the new concern—technical support—and has temporarily tabled the issue of money. Once the technical support concern is addressed, he or she will return to the negotiation discussion.

Of course, this is not what usually happens—the buyer, again, says "Yes" to this second question, just as he or she did the first. The salesperson is now ready to move to the third and final condition.

Question 3: Are the Buyers Ready to Commit?

Now that you have these two conditions in place, it is time for you to ask your buyers to make a commitment to do business as a condition of negotiating. This is a perfectly appropriate step; otherwise, what would be the point of the impending price discussion? You are entitled to a commitment from your buyer in exchange for a willingness to negotiate.

To get this commitment, ask this final question: "If we can get to an agreement on the price issue, are you ready to move forward?"

Notice the choice of words here: "If we can get to an agreement on the price issue" is not the same as saying "If I lower my price," and "are you ready to move forward?" is not the same as "will you buy today?" Your choice of words here is a very effective "soft" way to secure the commitment to buy.

"Your price is too high."
"I understand. If we set the price issue aside for a moment, is my
   recommendation what you want?
"Yes."
"Is price the only concern at this point?
"Yes."
"If we can get to agreement on the price issue, are you ready to
   move forward?
"Yes."

Now, you are ready to negotiate.

As you will see momentarily, we have no plans to reduce our fee—yet we can still get to a mutual agreement on the subject of price. The time to do so has now arrived—as has the time to ask one of the questions that we avoided earlier: "Too much by how much?" or "How far apart are we?" At this point, you must know what the difference is between what was quoted and where the client needs to be; otherwise, you don't have enough information to negotiate. For our purposes here, assume that the total investment you are asking for is $10,000. When you ask the client, "How far apart are we?" the response you get is, "We cannot go over $8,000." Now, you are ready to act.

Negotiate Your Recommendations, Not Your Pricing

The time has come for a basic accounting lesson; see Figure 10.2.

Figure 10.2

How to negotiate your recommendation.

In this figure, note "The Bottom Line." This is the total cost of your recommendations, and also represents your, and your company's, profit margin." *Profit* here is defined as the place where you get compensated for all the hard work that has brought you to this point in the competitive selling process. It also represents the place where your employer is compensated for the value that it will be providing the client.

On the left-hand side, we show "Value-Added Items." This is the listing of your recommendations, and is simply a summary of what things cost.

Here's the point: Your profit—the bottom-line figure—is off limits for negotiation; dominant predators do not work out agreements that are based on that number. The reason is simple: They do not allow their hard-earned income to become a bargaining chip in the negotiation process.

So what options do you have? You still have the same $2,000 problem—your recommendations cost $10,000, but the client can only spend the initial budgeted figure of $8,000. What's a dominant predator to do?

The answer is simple: Adjust the recommendations that you initially made to meet the figure needed by the client. In other words, offer to modify the proposal in a way that removes as little value as possible yet still meets the budget requirements of the client. This is why it is so important to make the optimal-solution proposal pricing your basis for negotiating; in a worst-case scenario, you modify this option to meet the stated budget—which accomplishes the ideal compromise. You maintain the profit margins that you are entitled to, and the buyers get the maximum amount of value available for their spending limit. This adjustment assumes, incidentally, that the buyers are "stuck" on their budget number. In many cases, this does not happen.

I deal with this issue on a regular basis; because my business is speaking to associations and corporate groups, the resource that I negotiate is my time. To cite one example, I had a prospective client who was considering my firm and two others; my initial proposal had been to conduct a three-day training program, which exceeded his budget. I recommended a three-day course because it was the best fit for his spectrum of needs regarding the training of his sales force; unfortunately, when I presented this option to the inner circle, the Spock of the group, an executive vice president of sales and marketing, said, "Well, this looks great, but it is out of our budget."

You already know what happened next: I began by asking, "If we remove the fee from my proposal, is the training program that I have recommended what you want?"

"Yes, but it's more than we can spend," she replied.

"Is that the only concern that you have with my proposal?"

"Yes, that's the only concern."

"I see. If we can get to agreement on the fee issue, are you ready to move forward with my training program for your group?"

"Yes. If we can work out the fee issue, we are ready to move forward."

I had two choices: (1) reduce my fee or (2) adjust my initial recommendation. You probably can guess what happened next: I offered a two-day version of the three-day course, met their budget requirements, and closed the deal. This gave them good value for their investment, satisfied their basic requirements, and protected my profit margin. Reducing my fee would have, in my case, required me to do free work—and that would not be fair to my other clients any more than it would be to yours.

Handling "We Need to Think This Over"

When you ask for feedback on your pricing, the other objection that will be raised—and, in a group decision, probably the most common one—is the *decision to postpone the decision*. This is understandable in such circumstances—the inner circle will feel that it cannot give you an immediate answer on your proposal recommendations without discussing them first—and besides, they can't read one another's minds. So you can expect a delay between the end of your presentation meeting and notification that they are ready to move forward.

This does not mean that you should do what most salespeople do, which is to thank them for their time, leave, and keep your fingers crossed. While you will not be able to close the deal in such a situation, you are entitled to know where you stand—and, if you handle this correctly, you can find out, with a high degree of accuracy, whether or not they are going to approve your proposal.

PREDATOR POINT

Ask the group which member is to be contacted for the final decision. Make sure that you have this person's direct extension and e-mail address.

As with the price objection, there are three consecutive questions that need to be asked, in exactly the following order and exactly as shown, to accomplish this objective.

Question 1: What Is the Time Frame?

Here, you will establish a deadline for the decision by asking a question and then providing your own answer: "How much time do you need to make your decision? If I follow up with you in three business days, would that be adequate?"

The importance of your following this "script" to the letter when requesting a deadline cannot be stressed enough because it enables you to set a firm date by which the decision will be made. The reason that this is so important is that adding a deadline to the decision makes it a priority for the inner circle. Decisions that have no deadline have a tendency to be put off, delayed, and sometimes completely forgotten. Establishing a date by which the group agrees to get to closure on your recommendations ensures that this decision will not be allowed to get buried under other day-to-day issues that inevitably arise.

You also will note that I suggested three business days; there are two reasons for this choice of timetable. First, the group will agree to virtually any reasonable time frame that you suggest, so suggest the shortest one possible. Second, you know that the group will forget 80 percent of what was discussed within a week of the meeting. Don't allow this inevitable lapse of memory to derail the value of your proposal. Strike while the iron is hot, and get a decision promptly.

Question 2: Is Anything Else Needed?
Next, you will want to verbally confirm with the inner circle that you have satisfied all the information requirements relative to the pending decision on your proposal. To do this, simply ask, "Do you have everything that you need at this point to make your decision?"

This question is a bit of a setup question. The group will respond with, "Yes, you've been very helpful." This admission that they are fully armed with the tools they need to decide the outcome opens the door for you to ask for a tentative commitment, which you will do now.

Question 3: Will They Ultimately Buy?
At this point, the inner circle has seen your complete recommendation, and they have been presented with your pricing—meaning that they have, as they just verbally confirmed, everything they need to

make a decision. You will now conduct a test—you will ask for a tentative commitment and find out where you stand relative to your winning the business. As with the other questions, it is important that you memorize, verbatim, the way in which the commitment question is asked: "Recognizing that you need a few days to make your decision, do you plan at this point to move forward with my proposal?"

Discussion of a Next Step

When you ask that last question, everyone on the committee will look at one person—the ranking person in the group. That person, usually the trigger, will respond to your question in one of two ways. The first will be a verbal commitment, such as the following:

"We plan to work with you, but first we need to discuss it."
"This is just what we need, but the committee needs to review it."
"We have a few details to work out, but you can plan on us
    moving forward."

This is known as a *conditional "Yes"*—a tentative commitment that hinges on a future event. If this is the response that you receive, you have an 80 percent or higher likelihood of closing the sale.

Any other response is a cause for concern—because *anything* other than a conditional "Yes" is a noncommital answer and indicates a 20 percent or less likelihood of closing. Examples:

"Well, we will just have to let you know."
"Just give us a call on Tuesday."
"We have to discuss it first."

This does not guarantee that you have a problem—but you should assume that you do. If you get such a noncommittal response, be paranoid—assume that there is a concern until you prove otherwise. Ask the group, "What concerns do you still have?" and see what you get for a response. Sometimes you may have someone raise a last-minute issue that had not been brought to your attention previously. If so, consider this good news—you found out about it before leaving the meeting. Address it, and then conclude. Otherwise, if no additional issues are raised, you should conclude the meeting.

Examples of both potential outcomes are shown below.

"We need to think this over."
"I understand. How much time do you need? Would three days be adequate?"
"Yes."
"Do you have everything that you need to make your decision on [date]?"
"Yes."
"Recognizing that you need until [date] to make your decision, do you plan at this point to move forward with my proposal?"

The 80% percent committal response:

"Yes, we plan to move forward, but first we need to _____."
This is the answer you are looking for; thank them for their time, and conclude the meeting. Follow up on the agreed-upon date.

The 20 percent commital response:

"Well, just call us on Tuesday, and we will let you know."
Assume that you have a problem! Respond with: "I will do that".
Then ask, "What concerns you at this point?"
Handle any objection raised as a result of this last question, and then conclude the meeting. Follow up on the agreed-upon date.

Asking for the Order

There are many ways to ask for the order; some are highly effective, some not so much, and some just plain stupid. One example of the latter—this is of the "do not try this at home" variety—is aptly named the "falling pen close." Here's how it works: You place your pen on the contract, extend the document to the buyer with the pen balanced precariously on top, and then—Chris Farley-style—exclaim "Whoopsie-daisy!" while allowing the pen to slide off the edge of the paper and fall to the floor. This "mistake" is followed up with a request: "I'm so clumsy. Would you mind reaching down and getting my pen for me?" By providing his or her assistance, the unwitting buyer ends up with the pen in his or her hand; when he or she comes up from beneath the desk, you immediately hold the contract in front of him or her and say, "Now, press hard. You are making multiple copies."

Yikes! No wonder closing has a bad reputation.

As stated earlier, an effective closing technique is one that makes it easy for your buyer to say, "Yes." If he or she is ready to move forward, what is needed is a way to reach out and gently bring him or her over to the other side.

Prerequisites for Closing

Before I discuss closing techniques, it is worth noting that every closing technique on the planet is useless if you do not have the following conditions in place at the time you ask for the order:

- The buyers have the financial ability to buy.
- The buyers have the authority to make the decision.
- The buyers want to do business with you.

Assuming that these conditions exist, you are ready to move forward.

The Calendar Close

Irrespective of whether you sell products or services, there usually will be a period of time between when the decision is formally made and when the next step takes place. Examples of these postsale steps can include

- Delivery of the ordered product
- Scheduling of software installation
- The first consulting meeting with the client
- Dates for conducting training
- The start date for the advertising program

When dealing with the inner circle group dynamic, as is usually the case when in a competitive sale, this situation provides you with a near-perfect method with which to close; you can use the "lag time" that occurs between when the decision is made and when the next postdecision event takes place as the basis for closing.

The *calendar close* uses this time period between the decision and the next step to ask for the order. Note that in each of the examples shown below, we never have to ask the buyer for their business; the calendar becomes the basis for that decision.

It has been my experience that we like to have ___ [days/weeks] from the time that you make your decision until the time that we [schedule the installation, make delivery, schedule the first run date, etc.].

With this in mind, today's date is _____, so counting forward ____ days from today puts us at [date] for a [delivery, installation, first run] date.

How does this day look on everyone's calendar?

Calendar Close Example: Product Sale

It has been my experience that we like to have two weeks from the time you place your order until the time that we deliver the product to your warehouse. With this in mind, today is October 14, so counting forward two weeks from today would put us at October 28 for a delivery date. Does this date work for you for the first delivery?

Calendar Close Example: Service Sale

It has been my experience that our technical group likes to have 30 days from the time that you make your decision until the time that we schedule our orientation meeting with your systems personnel. With this in mind, today is July 14, so we are looking at the week of August 12 for our next meeting. How does this week look on your calendar for scheduling the orientation date?

In most cases, if the client is ready to act, what you will see next is a discussion within the group regarding the date that you suggested, with the senior person "closing" the sale for you after overseeing input from the rest of the group. In both the preceding examples, if the client agrees to the date that you offer—or, for that matter, suggests a different one—the decision has been made. There is no longer the issue of "Yes" or "No," only "When." Immediately after reaching a verbal agreement on the next scheduled date, smile and say, "Thank you very much for your business. I am looking forward to working with you."

PREDATOR POINT

Never produce contracts or other paperwork during the closing process. All documents are post-decision, and follow the "thank you" or handshake.

Congratulations! You have won the competitive sale—and learned the entire selling process of the dominant predator. In Chapter 11 you will go on the offensive—and learn how to take accounts that belong to your competitors away from them.

Chapter | 11

BEHIND ENEMY LINES

How to Sell to the
Competitive User

In the preceding 10 chapters I outlined a strategy for winning competitive battles when a customer is actively seeking a solution provider and an opportunity therefore is "in play" among multiple vendors. However, dominant predators are not content with simply competing for the business of buyers who are actively shopping. They also grow their base of business by being skilled at actively pursuing and acquiring the clients of their competition. This chapter will review both short- and long-term strategies for methodically moving competitive users—the clients of competing firms—from their account base to yours.

PREDATOR POINT

You have little control over incoming calls from prospects. You have complete control over marketing to competitive users.

A Mistake to Avoid

Most salespeople have difficulty in taking business from competitors because their initial approach is not planned properly, and this failure to think long and hard before taking action defeats the salesperson's effort before it even begins. In most cases, it's because they don't respect the current relationship that exists and willfully ignore the political minefields involved in persuading a buyer to change vendors. They think that if they can just get their foot in the door and talk to the right person, they simply can yank the account away from their entrenched competitor. For those of you who think that this is an effective way to acquire competitive users as clients, I am the bearer of bad news: Speaking as a buyer myself, it just doesn't usually work that way. If you want to have real success in this arena, you first must broaden your understanding of the playing field, so I will begin by presenting the existing situation from the perspective of your competitor's customer.

Reasons for Encountering Immediate Resistance

"We're happy with our current vendor." This is the knee-jerk response that most competitive users have with regard to your initial inquiry about the existing relationship. The truth in this statement varies from one prospect to another; the important point is in understanding why the truthfulness of the statement really doesn't matter.

Unless this user of your competitor's products or services is having major problems, at this exact moment, with their existing vendor, he or she will react negatively to any overture seeking to change that relationship. In fact, any suggestion that you "replace" an existing supplier not currently in trouble will be met with immediate resistance, and from the user's perception, there are several practical reasons for this.

The first is that most inquiries of this nature are viewed initially as a threat because of the issue of familiarity. Your competitor is a "known" entity to the competitive user, whereas you are not. Therefore, there is a significant level of perceived risk in leaving the safety of an established relationship for a new one. What if you don't match the service of the current supplier? What if you don't keep your promises? What if this turns out to be a mistake? The safest decision therefore is to stay put, irrespective of what your firm claims to offer.

Second, there is the issue of loyalty. As a business owner, I can tell you that ending a relationship with an established vendor is not really that different from firing an employee—it can be a stressful, unpleasant task that most people, given a choice, would prefer to avoid. In cases where the existing supplier is providing a satisfactory level of service, this point alone is enough to warrant dismissing your efforts out of hand.

Third, there is the simple inconvenience of everything that is involved in starting over with a new vendor. New people. New processes. New procedures. Major headache! Your competitive user needs to have a good reason for going through the grind of changing suppliers. Have you given him or her one?

Saving Money Is Not Enough

When making their initial approach, the default strategy for most salespeople is to ignore all these factors. Instead, they simply dangle a lower price in front of the competitive user. "We will save you money!" is the usual pitch. There are two problems with this selling strategy. First, you are presenting what you are offering as an apples-to-apples commodity and nothing more. There is no offer of any real value in what you propose; it is perceived to be simply the same thing for less money. Second, if you are in a competitive business, your pricing is not likely to differ so much from your competition that it would provide a level of savings sufficient to offset the aggravation of changing vendors.

> ## PREDATOR POINT
> Dominant predators use superior value, not a lower price, to persuade competitive users to change vendors.

I can give you a current example in my business to illustrate this point. I have been a loyal customer of a payroll services firm that I have been using for 12 years now. The company provides a mundane but necessary service to my company. It performs perfectly adequately for my needs, and I have never had any significant problem with its service. In fact, the relationship has been trouble-free, which is exactly how I like my vendor relationships to be.

One of the company's competitors has approached me recently and wants me to meet with him to discuss possibly leaving my current supplier for his firm; the lone "carrot" I am being offered here is that he claims to cost less.

This may well be the case, but so what? I am getting good service from the firm I am using, it isn't costly to begin with, and I am not having any problems with the current provider. In addition, leaving my current service for this new one will take up a considerable amount of my time to do—and I am very busy at the moment with other things, such as writing this book. Why would I want to go through the inconvenience of changing this area of my business to save a few bucks? I have no reason to believe that the offerings of the new firm would not serve me well; in this case, the risk issue is not a factor in the slightest. The fact is that I have a large number of more pressing issues to contend with, I have nothing significant to gain by making the change, and taking this step would be a huge hassle. This is not to say that I wouldn't consider changing vendors, but I would need something more substantial than a marginally lower price for doing so.

Short-Term Strategy and Long-Term Strategy

Now that we have established that, in most cases, quickly and completely replacing an existing vendor without just cause is an unrealistic objective, you need to have both a short-term and a long-term strategy for acquiring the accounts of your competitors.

Short-Term Strategy: Supplementing and Sampling

I define *short-term* here as opportunities that you have determined can realistically make a vendor change to you within six months or less and *long-term* as those that will take six months or longer. If you are in a service-based business, the best short-term strategy is to approach the prospective account with the ability to act as a supplemental, or secondary, provider. This means that your immediate goal is to first establish a relationship that supplements, but does not replace, the existing one with your competitor. While this strategy may not provide the immediate payoff that you get from replacing a competitor outright, it does provide you with a way to get your foot in the door. It also allows you the opportunity, in time, to prove your superiority so that you can replace the competitor later. Most important, the company will be much more receptive to the idea of working with you in this way because you do not threaten the existing relationship.

One of the largest accounts that I acquired in my sales training days was closed in exactly this manner. The company I had approached was using the services of one of my competitors for all its sales force development needs. When I made my initial inquiry, I was told, of course, that the company was very happy with who it was using.

Undeterred, I went directly to the decision maker and persuaded her to have me supplement the existing course offering by conducting a half-day workshop for the sales team on advanced prospecting skills during its annual sales conference. This gave the client an opportunity to "kick my tires" and compare the quality of my work with that of the existing vendor. In short order, I completely replaced the current firm—and I learned that contrary to what I was told initially, the company had not been "happy" at all with what the other trainer had been providing. Frequently, in such situations, you will hear the same thing.

Of course, success with this tactic requires that you have something to offer—a "killer app," if you will—that will get the attention of the competitive user. This offering needs to be a resource that the customer needs but is either not getting from your competitor at all or is getting but is having less than satisfactory results. Be creative, make sure that you understand exactly what your competitor is currently providing, and offer something unique and different. Once you determine what this supplemental service will be, you end up making it easy for the buyer to work with you. Often, this is all it takes to get the ball rolling.

If you sell a tangible product, getting the client to sample what you offer as a point of comparison is a similar, and equally effective, short-term strategy. However, when approaching the competitive user with the offer of a trial or sample, do not make the mistake of offering it for free! This is a cardinal sin when it comes to tangible products. Many salespeople with whom I have worked over the years were in the habit of providing a "free" sample of their products to competitive users, with no cost or obligation of any kind. This is an expensive, redundant mistake that virtually guarantees that the item provided will not be used by the buyer.

There are two problems with this bad habit. The first is that when you ask a buyer the question, "Would you like to try this at no cost?" it is easier to say yes than no. This means that hordes of buyers who have no interest in what you have will gladly say "Yes" to your offer to get you out of their office. Second, if there is no "skin in the game" on the buyer's part, and there are therefore no negative consequences to doing nothing with your free sample, what motivation does the buyer possibly have for actually using it? Because of this, the result of the free offer is almost always the same: The item goes on a shelf with all the other "freebies" that gather dust, sometimes for years, on top of a filing cabinet, representing a material cost to the seller and an unsightly paperweight to the recipient.

Instead, when you offer a sample item, only do so if you determine that there is a real and legitimate potential value to the competitive user. Then ask the prospective client to pay a nominal fee that represents the value of the sample that you are providing. This isn't an issue of money; the amount should be small, and it is largely irrelevant. Rather, the real issue here is one of qualifying your buyer. Put another way, if the competitive user isn't interested enough in what you offer to pay a token price for a small sample of it, he or she is not remotely interested in doing business with you in the first place, and this entire exercise is, at the present time, a complete waste of your time and the company's resources.

PREDATOR POINT

The "sweet spot" amount to charge for a product to sample is between $49 and $100.

Asking for a nominal fee for any sample of what you provide is therefore a highly effective strategy for both qualifying the interest level of competitive users and managing your time more efficiently. When money changes hands, the competitive user has a stake in the outcome—and therefore is motivated to give your product the trial use that it deserves. In addition, don't overlook the fact that you have now established a buyer-seller relationship, complete with a customer number and invoice. This formality makes it that much easier for the buyer to place a larger future order if the sample performs to expectations, don't you agree?

Long-Term Strategy: Timing and Branding

Supplementing and sampling are short-term ways to initiate and build relationships with competitive users. However, if you want to have real growth in market share at the expense of your competitors, you need to design and follow a marketing strategy that is effective in breaking down barriers created by your entrenched competitors. This requires that you first understand and respect the roles of timing and branding as they pertain to changing vendors.

The process that I addressed in the first 10 chapters of this book materializes when buyers recognize a need within their organization and call on you and your peers to compete for their business. Neither you nor your competitors prompted that situation, nor did any of you have a role in its initiation or development. Nevertheless, when this happened, a temporary window of opportunity opened for you and your competition—temporary because once the buyers selected you to fill that need, the window was, for the time being, at least, closed again.

When it comes to competitive users changing vendors, timing is the key variable in opportunities for winning business. You cannot control when one of your competitive users is ready to entertain the idea of switching—but you can heavily influence who gets the phone call when that decision is made. The key is branding—creating top-of-mind awareness among the competitive users within your market and educating these people on your firm and what you offer.

> **PREDATOR POINT**
>
> Dominant predators recognize that real success in this area comes from a combination of strategy, patience, and persistence.

The Importance of Branding to Your Long-Term Strategy

Several summers ago I was at home one evening reading a magazine in bed. Out of the corner of my eye, I noticed that a large insect was marching across the foot of the bedspread. This caused me to drop the magazine. On closer inspection, I saw that it appeared to be a large ant with wings. There is only one insect that I knew of that looked like a large ant with wings. That insect is a termite.

Now, prior to this event, I had absolutely no interest whatsoever in pest control services. However, when the winged ant appeared on my bedspread, the timing factor kicked in—and a window of opportunity opened for the pest control industry. Keep in mind that the appearance of that insect in my home was an event that was not influenced in any way by any vendor of those services.

As you would expect, I immediately did a Web search for local pest control firms to address my newly found and immediate need. My search produced two businesses with local offices. The first, which I will call MegaBug, was a name that you would immediately recognize because it was a national company that has spent gazillions of dollars building its brand and therefore is the first company you think of when you think of pest control services. The second one I will call Bugg Busters—a firm that, like you, I had never heard of.

Armed with the names of these two competitors, I did the same thing that anyone else would do—I called MegaBug simply because I recognized the name. Keep in mind that there was no logical reason for me to pick MegaBug over Bugg Busters; people buy from who they "know," and MegaBug was known to me, whereas Bugg Busters was not. (There is that risk issue again.)

A MegaBug employee came to my house; on his arrival, I provided him with the reason for the phone call in a small mason jar. He set the culprit down on the kitchen counter and proceeded with a full inspection of the premises. At the conclusion of his assessment, I got some good news: The insect that I had captured was, in fact, a carpenter ant—meaning that I did not have a termite infestation.

However, as Mr. MegaBug was quick to point out, I was completely defenseless and vulnerable to a massive termite infestation at any time. The man was a master at building drama into his sales presentation; by the time he finished, I could visualize an entire battalion of the little beasts poised by my mailbox with battle streamers, tanks, and heavy artillery. He then made his recommendation: I needed to spend over $10,000 on an elaborate baiting system his company offered that was guaranteed to prevent me from ever having termites. That sounded great, except for one little caveat: It seemed a bit of—no pun intended—overkill because I didn't have any termites to begin with. Since this was the only solution that he offered, I told him I wanted to "think it over"—and on his departure I went to plan B—I called Bugg Busters.

It is important to note here that the only reason Bugg Busters got the opportunity to earn my business was because their national-brand competitor tried to unnecessarily oversell me with a solution to a problem that I did not have. In fact, Bugg Busters simply got lucky—the brand name dropped the ball by trying to oversell me, and the unknown entity got a shot at my business. In short order, a Bugg Busters employee came to the house, arrived at the same conclusion that MegaBug had—and then recommended a twice-a-year liquid treatment as a preventative measure for a fraction of the cost of the MegaBug program. I accepted his proposal and have been a happy, termite-free customer of Bugg Busters ever since.

In any competitive business, including yours, there are players that are MegaBugs, and there are those that are Bugg Busters. When it comes to selling to the competitive user, the most important issue that you need to address is this: Are you MegaBug or Bugg Busters to these key accounts? Do they know who you are—do they know you by name? Are they educated—familiar with your company and the full spectrum of what you provide? Do you have instant name recognition? Or are you, as Bugg Busters was to me, a nobody—a complete stranger?

When timing caused me to be in the market for pest control services, MegaBug got the invitation to sell simply because I recognized its name. If you want to take business away from your competitors, the name of the game here is *branding*. You must employ a long-term marketing strategy that builds top-of-mind awareness for your business with the inner circle members to whom you wish to sell.

Marketing to the Competitive User

When it comes to pursuing these competitive user accounts, the hallmark of the dominant predator is *consistency*. Brand recognition does not occur overnight—but it doesn't have to take years to establish either. As with the other skills outlined in this book, nothing is more effective than implementing and following a proven methodology. In this case, the methodology involves a combination of planning, patience, and software—specifically, contact management software—to create top-of-mind awareness among the competitive users in your market. For a salesperson working in a territory or market, this is known as *microbranding* because your efforts are targeted to a small percentage of the market—in this case, only the companies that use the products and services of your competitors.

The first step in this process involves the separation of "wheat from chaff"—segregating the competitive users in your market from all the other prospects you pursue. In other words, if a business within your market uses one of your competitors, it automatically is pulled from the market and placed in a separate category to receive special attention.

The easiest way to store and manage these accounts is through the use of an off-the-shelf contact management software program, such as ACT!™, Maximizer™, or Goldmine™. If you have an internal database management system, it is likely that your existing program can serve in this capacity as well. Once you have loaded the software, create a special database just for this purpose and name it "Competitive Users." As you identify customers of your competitors' products and/or services, these accounts get "pulled" from your territory or market and added to this exclusive "Competitive Users" database.

In addition to basic information for each of these accounts, you will need to identify the members of their inner circle, as outlined in Chapter 4.

PREDATOR POINT

The most important contacts of the Competitive User account are those with a vested interest in the performance of your competitor.

There are numerous resources available for obtaining this information, including

- Company Web sites
- List marketers, such as "Best Lists"
- Trade publications
- Chamber of commerce directories
- Old-fashioned cold calls

As you uncover these competitive-user accounts, gathering and storing the names and titles of all inner circle members becomes your first priority. The reason is that when an opportunity for vendor change arises, you want all these people to know who you are and what your value proposition is so that when the termite crawls across the proverbial bedspread, you will be "known" to every one of them.

Selling to the Competitive User

With these accounts, brand awareness is accomplished through *spaced-repetition marketing*. This means that you will be contacting them on a schedule. Your frequency of contact should be bimonthly, meaning that each person on your database will receive a call from you every eight weeks. This is frequent enough to keep your company on their radar screen without being considered a pest. There are two ways to ensure that this gets accomplished. The first, and more difficult to execute, is to block time out to contact every one of them once every two months during a single prospecting session.

A more practical method that involves a little extra initial work but is much easier to administer is to divide your competitive users into eight subsets in the database using one of the custom fields available in the software. Label this field "Group __," and then designate each member of the first set of competitive users as being in "Group A," the second as "Group B," etc. until you complete the setup with the eighth and final set as "Group H."

Once this is accomplished, your weekly routine will include calling, on an eight-week rotation, each group of competitive users at the rate of one group per week. This is an easy habit to get into each week and requires much less time from your regular schedule—and ensures that every person in your "Competitive User" database gets contacted every two months. As with all prospecting inquires, you must be skilled at dealing with two people at competitive user accounts: the gatekeeper and the key contact.

Making the Initial Call

Let's take a look at how to properly approach these two people, armed with the information in your database.

The Gatekeeper

Gatekeepers, if handled properly, are not the obstacle that most salespeople think they are. The key to working with gatekeepers is to treat them with the respect and courtesy they deserve. This means that you are polite, courteous, and state your business as soon as they take your call. Keep in mind that you are not selling on the phone when making this call; you are simply making an inquiry, given the fact that this company uses the types of products and/or services that you provide.

Gatekeepers at competitive user accounts need to have answers to three specific questions before they can act on your call and respond proactively to your request. In order, these are

1. Who are you?

2. What is the call regarding?

3. With whom do you wish to speak?

It is important to note here that because you are maintaining information on these accounts in a database that is updated every eight weeks, you will have the name of the person with whom you wish to speak, as well as know the name of your competitor who services this account. Now, proper planning and good information management combine to pay big dividends. When you make contact with the gatekeeper, you can effortlessly deliver the three pieces of information they require in the following manner:

1. *Who are you?* "Hi, this is [your name] with [your company]."
2. *What is the call regarding?* "The reason I am calling is that I had a question for [key contact] regarding the products/services your firm uses with [name of competitor]."
3. *With whom do you wish to speak?* "Is [key contact] available, please?"

Wait for the gatekeeper to respond. Because you are knowledgeable of the company and have a good business reason for calling, this "script" will provide you with a high success rate in being put through to your key contact.

The Key Contact

Like the gatekeeper, the key contact at the competitive-user account needs to know the answers to three questions of his or her own when he or she answers the telephone. In order, these are

1. Who are you?
2. What's in it for me?
3. What do you want?

As with the gatekeeper, you use the same information about the account to state your business:

1. *Who are you?* "Hi, this is [your name] with [your company]."
2. *What's in it for me?* "The reason I called is in regard to your relationship with [competitor]. My firm provides a specialized [product/service] that has helped other customers of [competitor] to [benefit—reduce operating expenses, improve product quality, etc.].
3. *What do you want?* "I am calling to request a brief meeting with you to discuss what we offer in this area in more detail. How does your schedule look for a half-hour meeting during the week of _____?"

Handling Immediate Resistance

"We are happy with our current vendor." As mentioned earlier in this chapter, this is the universal objection of the competitive user. Remember that your best approach to the competitive user is to supplement, not replace, his or her current supplier. Therefore, you will handle the objection as follows:

> I understand, but it is very likely that we can supplement what you currently do with [competitor] without affecting that relationship and give you additional value in the process. As I mentioned, I will keep this to thirty minutes and will make sure that the meeting is a worthwhile investment of your time. Is there a day during the week of _____ that works best for you?

This is a logical and perfectly sound reason for having an exploratory meeting—and in many cases, your competitive user will agree to see you. In fact, you should experience an ongoing close rate of one appointment for every eight to ten contacted prospects—a close rate in the neighborhood of 15 percent.

The effect of this marketing system, if you stick with it, will astound you. While the immediate goal—and benefit—of making these calls is to set appointments with these prospects, consider the impact that contacting these people every eight weeks—six times a year—has on the issue of brand awareness. In a year's time, competitive users who know nothing of you today will, 12 months from now, know who you are, know what your company does, and be thoroughly educated on your value proposition—all because of your spaced-repetition approach to marketing. The reason that this is so important is because of the timing factor. Now, this issue that you have no control over works to your benefit. Whenever the day comes—and it will, sooner or later—when a change of supplier is required, you will be a known resource, and when the window of opportunity opens, you will receive a phone call. Best of all, even if you are one of several options being considered, you will be dealing with an inner circle group whose members all have had prior contact with you, know who you are, and are well aware of your desire to earn their business.

PREDATOR POINT

Making weekly prospecting calls to your Competitive User list will provide you with a steady and dependable source of leads.

Following this weekly process takes commitment, focus, and self-discipline. You must plan time out of your week, preferably at the same time every week, for this purpose. However, the benefits of methodically pursuing competitive users are huge. You will keep your calendar full of appointments, but more important, you will generate a consistent flow of quality leads—all from businesses who already use types of products and services that you sell and therefore are easier to close than those "cold" prospects who do not.

The Competitive-User Needs Analysis

Once you have successfully secured an appointment with the competitive user, you will follow the same fundamental selling process that you covered in the first 10 chapters of this book. The only significant variation here is found within the client needs analysis.

Because this is an account in which you have an entrenched competitor, the focus of your questions naturally will center on the relationship that the prospect has with your competitor's company. This is not to say that you will ignore other aspects of the prospective client's business, but your opportunity here obviously depends heavily on finding "gaps" between the company's expectations of your competitor and the competitor's ability, to date, to meet those expectations. With this in mind, your list of topic-opening questions—your needles in the haystack—surely would include the following:

- History of the relationship with the competitor
- What the competitor currently provides your potential client
- What the competitor does not provide that your potential client wants
- What your potential client likes most about your competition
- What your potential client likes least about your competition
- What, if any, turnover your potential client has experienced with sales reps
- The technical skill and dependability of the current sales rep servicing the account

- What your potential client would most like to improve regarding the current relationship
- What would motivate your potential client to consider changing vendors

Don't be afraid to ask that last question—it shows the prospect that you are seriously interested in his or her company and that you mean business. After the needs analysis, the sales process—accessing the inner circle, interviewing, presenting solutions, and closing—mirrors that covered in Chapters 1 through 10.

A Final Note

This is an environment where you will regularly hear negative things about your competitors. Remember the point made in Chapter 7 about bad-mouthing your competition: Always refrain, even if invited to do so during a meeting with the influencer. When the customer makes negative comments about your competitor, it's an invitation for you to come in and replace that competitor. However, you are doing nothing to improve your chances by joining the fray. Instead, maintain your professionalism. This position will serve you well at the time that the final decision to change is made.

Chapter | 12

IT IS WHAT IT IS

How the Ordinary Become Extraordinary

In their landmark study of wealth in America, *The Millionaire Next Door*, authors Thomas Stanley and William Danko interviewed over 700 people with a net worth in excess of $1 million to determine what the characteristics are of individuals who attain financial success. One of the most interesting facts that I learned from this book is that most wealthy people fall into one of four occupations. These are business owners, doctors, lawyers, and . . . salespeople. Research therefore has established that you have chosen a high-income occupation. If you have read to this point in this book, you either are or sincerely want to be one of these people. As a thank-you for the time that you have invested, this last chapter is designed to be a bonus for you—a personal coaching session that will show you what it takes to join their ranks.

Natural Ability Versus Skill

The 80/20 rule, or the Pareto principle, states that roughly 80 percent of the effects of any event come from 20 percent of the causes. When it comes to successful selling, you already know that this principle applies to our profession as well—that 80 percent of sales revenue really *is* "caused" by 20 percent of the salespeople doing the selling—those whom I refer to in this book as dominant predators. Those top 20 percent are also the ones who get all the "goodies" that everyone who chooses a sales career wants—the high income, the promotions, the stock options, etc. What most of us don't stop to consider is this: If 20 percent of the salespeople really do make 80 percent of the money to be made in the sales profession, that also would mean that the remaining 80 percent of salespeople get to fight for the scraps that are left over. Everybody who chooses a sales career wants to be in the top 20 percent; nobody ever chose a sales career because they yearn to be mediocre. Yet only one in five surpasses mediocrity. What do those people do or have that the other 80 percent do not?

Many people believe that the ability to sell is a natural one; hence the concept of the *born* salesperson. If the definition of an effective sales person is simply one who tells jokes, schmoozes people, and has the gift of gab—in other words, if there really isn't any skill involved in selling—then, certainly, that definition is accurate.

If you happen to be one of those people with this perception of salespeople, you might then assume that if I interviewed 100 sales reps, I could, without asking any questions about past sales performance, pick out the top 20 percent of such a group with some accuracy. In fact, I would not have a clue. This is due to the fact that the vast majority of people in sales careers already have the natural traits— being presentable, possessing good communication skills, and having the right personality—to be successful. Trying to randomly pick high achievers out of such a homogeneous group therefore is an exercise in futility. So, if most people in sales have the natural ability to be top performers, why do so few actually do it?

This book tackles just one aspect of a salesperson's job—that of competing successfully for business—and it took 11 chapters of material to review the skills required for just doing *that*. I would therefore make a strong argument that there is a significant amount of skill involved in becoming a high-income salesperson. In fact, I will go so far as to say that there is not an occupation in the world of business that requires more skill than that of a salesperson. If skill—and not natural ability—is the key to success in sales, then high achievers in sales are not gifted; they are highly skilled. So a better question to ask is, "How do the high achievers of sales acquire the skills they use to be so successful?"

PREDATOR POINT

Efficiency is the name of the game in the sales profession. The more skilled you are, the better the return on the time you invest.

The Mastery Grid

One of my peers in the speaking business is Jim Cathcart. He is a true leader within my profession, a superb speaker and sales trainer and the author of two excellent books, *Solution Selling* and *The Acorn Principle* (www.Cathcart.com). His concept, the "Mastery Grid," provides the best resource that I have seen to explain why some salespeople become high achievers and most do not (see Figure 12.1).

Figure 12.1

Successful salespeople and the 80/20 rule.

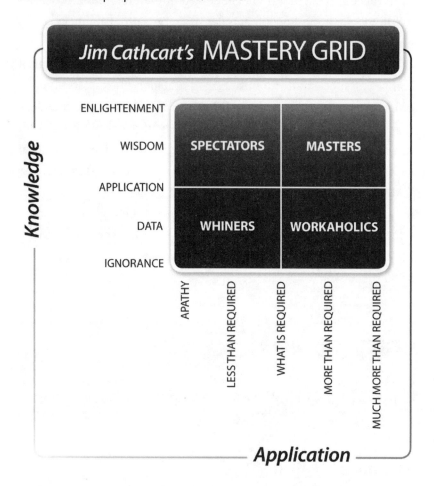

As you can see from the figure, there are two primary drivers for success in sales: down the left side, we have "Knowledge,"—what you know—and across the bottom, we have "Application," which is what you do with what you know. In my experience, every salesperson will rise to a point along both these grids and then tend to plateau or stop growing. The point at which the salesperson does this is the primary determinant of success, as you shall see later in this chapter.

How Much Do You Know?

With regard to the knowledge side of this grid, there are two types that are critical for salespeople—technical knowledge, which represents your depth of information regarding the products and services that you sell, and sales knowledge, which is the level of skill that you have acquired in the selling process. You can see that the low end of the "Knowledge" axis is "Ignorance"—not knowing anything. Every salesperson remembers their first day on the job; ignorance is the starting point of knowledge for every new salesperson.

From there, we move up the "Knowledge" graph to the next level, "Data." At this point on the grid, you are still a neophyte, but now you know enough to be dangerous. This is where you will find most salespeople who are still in their first year of employment. This salesperson has learned enough to do the fundamentals of the job—he or she has established a comfort zone in which he or she knows enough to function somewhat effectively, handling simple orders and answering basic questions about products and services. As long as he or she stays within his or her zone of comfort, all is well. However, if one of those tough Spock buyers from Chapter 4 asks a data-level salesperson a series of complex questions about items with which they are not yet familiar, the standard response from the sales rep is, of course, "I don't know, but I will find out and get back to you." Like the "Ignorance" level, "Data" is a step along the way for the sales trainee. We all go through this step in the course of a new role—it's part of the learning curve. Up to this point, everyone gets a free pass.

Then, however, we get to a very important spot on the "Knowledge" grid—"Competence." When you reach the "Competence" level of

"Knowledge" as a salesperson, you know enough to be effective at work, to make your sales quota, to keep your boss off your back, and to pay your mortgage—in short, to be comfortable in life. There is nothing wrong with any of this, but the subject of this final chapter is what it takes for high sales achievement. With this in mind, here is the cold, hard reality of the relationship among salespeople, knowledge, and success: For fully 80 percent of salespeople, when it comes to knowledge, competence is enough. Competence provides them with what they need to know to make a comfortable living, and when you get right down to it, that is all that they really want. They have learned enough to do the job adequately, and so they permanently plateau—they stop working on their education. They become average salespeople who make average incomes. This is neither good nor bad—it is what it is.

With regard to the issue of knowledge, if you are looking for the high achievers in sales, you will find virtually all of them clustered at the next level on the grid—"Wisdom." When a salesperson reaches the "Wisdom" level of "Knowledge," he or she knows more about his or her products and services and how to sell them effectively than 80 percent of other salespeople. The result of this information base is immediately evident when you encounter these salespeople. These are the "go-to" reps for the rest of the sales team, the informal experts to whom others gravitate, because they research all the questions and therefore have all of the answers. They are natural leaders—and are also the organization's future sales managers and executives. Customers value their time with these salespeople as well because they are a walking, talking source of information on industry trends, new technology, and new ideas. If you are a salesperson, you know who these people are in your company; perhaps you are one of them.

How did the "Wisdom" group gain the higher ground when it comes to knowledge? It isn't because they are smarter than everyone else; you don't have to be brilliant to be highly successful in sales or any other career. These people are simply better educated because they are seekers of new information. They look at their job as more of a calling than an occupation, and they are consumed with "what's new" both in their industry and in their profession. They read constantly—trade publications, books on sales, and industry magazines. They purchase audio learning programs and listen to them during drive time while their less successful peers listen to talk-show blather on the radio. They attend training seminars and other opportunities for learning and spend their own money to do it. In short, they are on a quest for continuous improvement.

As a sales trainer, one of the things that has always fascinated me about the relationship between salespeople and learning is that the most successful reps in any group with which I work—that is, those who need training the least—are always the ones that get the most benefit from it, whereas the ones who need it the most—the average performers—are also the ones who do the least with what they learn and therefore get the least return on the learning time invested. Case in point: I once gave a lengthy exam to a group of about 100 sales-people, all employed by a client for whom I had designed and presented a three-day sales training course. When the tests were graded, one sales person made a 99 on the test—the highest grade in the class and a near-perfect score. This was quite an accomplishment because the test was not easy—a combination of multiple-choice and discussion questions totaling 15 pages.

So, regarding that sales test, would you like to venture a guess as to the performance ranking of the salesperson who made the highest test score out of 100 participants? The answer, of course, is that he was the one who was already the perennial top producer in the company—for five years in a row, no less—which also made him the one person who needed to make a 99 the *least* of the 100 people who took the exam.

Why did this happen? Why does the value of new learning always benefit those who need it the least? The answer is this: Like most high achievers, he is on a perpetual quest for personal improvement. He found value in the material being presented, and as he does with everything else in his life, he was committed to getting the most out of the experience.

PREDATOR POINT

When attending sales training seminars, pick the three best ideas from the program, and master only those three before you work on anything else.

To conclude our review of the Knowledge side of the Grid, at the very top we have "Enlightenment," which, practically speaking, is an unnecessary level for salespeople to aspire to. This is so because at this level your education surpasses that of 97 percent of your peers. This is not needed for success and therefore is, for our purposes, a waste of time to attain.

Accordingly, to become a high achiever, you must be committed to attaining the wisdom level of knowledge, the equivalent of a master's degree in the sales profession. Now let's take a look at the other half of the equation—your commitment to action.

How Much Do You *Do*?

Along the bottom of the Mastery Grid we have "Application," which represents your work ethic—what you actually do to attain success. The starting point for "Application" is "Apathy," which represents doing nothing, just as ignorance represents knowing nothing. From there, we move to the right until we reach the point that represents doing "Less Than Required," which is another way to describe a salesperson who is lazy. Next, we arrive at the key point of "Application"—doing what is necessary. In other words, working hard enough to do your job, to make your sales quota, to keep your boss off your back, to pay your mortgage—in short, to be comfortable in life. And, as we did with "Competence," we arrive at the work ethic that represents 80 percent of all salespeople.

This, like competence, is not good or bad. It is what it is.

To illustrate: During one year in my business, I had the opportunity to ride in the field with five different salespeople, in different industries, who all had one thing in common—all had made a half-million dollars or more in personal income the previous year, in U.S. dollars, as a commissioned salesperson. One of these individuals, selling corrugated boxes in southern California, had earned, in commissions, $1.2 million during the previous year. I asked these superachievers a lot of questions (including, "Do you have any job openings, by chance?") in an attempt to better understand what it takes to reach this level of income as a salesperson. Among the questions I asked was this: "When do you come in every morning, and at what time of the day do you normally leave?" The collective answer—they were all within a half-hour of one another—might surprise you.

None of these individuals worked 80 hours a week; in fact, they put in no more than a full day every day—but they were focused, and they followed a strict routine. Here is their daily success formula: They were productive every day by 8 o'clock in the morning, and they finished their day at 6 p.m. each evening—occasionally even 6:30—but they were not starting their day at the crack of dawn and working long into the night either.

Compare this work ethic with the typical day for average-performing salespeople. In my experience, most salespeople are not productive until after 9 a.m., and most also turn the lights out, for all intents and purposes, around 4 o'clock in the afternoon. Nine to four versus eight to six—not a significant difference in time invested but an astounding difference in productivity.

These half-dozen superstars represent the next level on the "Application" grid—doing "More Than Required." Putting in just a few hours a day more than their peers enables these sales wizards to reap huge rewards. Where we don't find the heavy hitters is at "Much More Than Required"—the definition of having your life out of balance, that 80-hour work week—which is neither desirable nor necessary.

As you examine the diagram, it is worth noting that the difference between average performance and superachievement in sales when it comes to both knowledge and application is not a great leap but rather one step further along both grids. In other words, a small extra effort in learning and execution produces all the result that is necessary for high achievement as a salesperson.

Given that the two drivers for sales success are what you know and what you do with what you know, we can categorize all salespeople as being members of one of four different and distinct groups. The first group, in the lower left-hand corner of the grid, consists of the "Whiners," which, in my estimation, are a small percentage of the population, with roughly 10 percent of all salespeople falling into this group.

The Whiners

It is important to make a distinction here between "true" whiners and good sales reps who are simply high maintenance. Some of my best salespeople as a manager were world-class whiners when it came to complaining, foot stomping, cursing, and throwing general temper tantrums—but they also were high producers, which made my tolerance level for their behavior virtually limitless as well.

True whiners—the group shown here—are a different breed altogether. They are not getting it done, nor do they have any desire to get it done, and when you ask them why they are underachieving, their reasons all have one common denominator—it's always somebody else's fault. Because they place the blame for subpar performance on a range of factors that do not include themselves, they refuse to take ownership for their own success, so failure to succeed becomes a foregone conclusion.

To cite a recent example: One of the project-related services that I have provided for clients from time to time is to "camp out" with their sales force for an extended time, usually several consecutive weeks, to work with both the sales management team and the staff. As part of this relationship, I make myself available to go on field sales calls with the outside reps so that I can give them coaching assistance. Since I will completely run the sales call while the rep simply watches, they don't have to worry about "performing" in front of me. All that the reps have to do to schedule a ride with me is write down the time for the appointment on a posted sign-up sheet; I then check the calendar and schedule accordingly.

The moment that the sign-up sheet is posted in the sales department, the reps always immediately "morph" into two groups—the tigers and the turtles.

Tigers, which usually represent—surprise!—the top 20 percent of the team's current performers, aggressively monopolize my available field time. They will pester me for assistance, ask lots of questions, and take advantage of every available opportunity to work together in the field.

Turtles, on the other hand, slowly extend their heads over the top of their cubicles whenever I am in the sales area, just to eye level—high enough to see if I might be lurking nearby. If this is indeed the case, they immediately duck back into their cubicle "shells" until the threat has passed—otherwise, they might have to go on a sales call with me and actually learn something. It should come as no surprise that the turtles are also the group that needs outside assistance the most because they are usually underperforming, whereas the tigers are already doing well, need my assistance the least, but want to do better.

One such turtle was a young lady who had been in her current role for over a year, had never, during her entire time of employment, been above her sales quota, and had behaved as if I had leprosy from the moment I arrived in the office. I finally went to her sales manager and asked him, point blank, what his plans were regarding this woman, who I will call Gina.

"Oh, you just don't know her!" he explained. "She's actually a very nice person."

"I am sure that she is a *delightful* person," I replied. "But that has nothing to do with the fact that she has no interest in succeeding. What are you going to do about the situation with Gina?"

"Let me talk to her," replied the manager. Shortly thereafter, he met with Gina, and soon she was headed for a morning of sales calls with me. Her heels seemed to dig trenches across the parking lot, such was the extreme reluctance with which she accompanied her sales manager to her automobile. I could already tell that it was going to be a fun morning.

In the course of the next three and a half hours, I do not exaggerate when I tell you that Gina, who talked, nonstop, during our entire morning together, had no less than 36 different reasons for why she was struggling as a salesperson. It was the company, it was the territory, it was her manager, it was customer service, it was the competition, it was . . . everything you can imagine except that not once during this entire manifesto did she use the pronoun *I* in a single sentence—as in

"I need to ___." It was evident to me that Gina probably was not going to be successful, and it had nothing to do with her ability. It was her refusal to take any ownership for her own success that virtually guaranteed her failure. Shortly thereafter, she resigned her position with the company and found new employment. I have no doubt that the same external forces that conspired to keep her from being successful at her previous employer continue to plague her in her work with the current one.

PREDATOR POINT

Many external factors can negatively affect your performance. Dominant predators find a way to overcome them, and toss them aside.

The Workaholics

The next group on the Mastery Grid—a slightly larger one, representing roughly 20 percent of the sales population, in my estimation—consists of the "Workaholics." Unlike whiners, workaholics have a very desirable attribute—as you can see on the grid, they are way out on the "Application" arm; they possess a great work ethic. If fact, they put in long hours on a regular basis. Where they are sorely lacking is in the "Knowledge" area—the classic example of working hard but not working smart. Workaholics are great employees who are overworked and underpaid. They toil away for low wages because they are afraid of one thing—change. They continue to do the same old things in the same old way, refusing to adapt to new and potentially better ideas. Eventually, most workaholics get run over by competitors who are more knowledgeable and therefore run a more efficient business than they do.

An example of this refusal to adapt can be seen in the use of technology in territory or account management. The workaholic is the salesperson who says, "I don't need one of those laptops you people carry around with you to manage your customer base; I still use my shoebox full of three-by-five cards, and it serves me well, just as it has since I began selling in 1976. Plus, it's alphabetically sorted." Thus armed, they press on—and the travesty is that they have to work harder and harder to keep up with people who, in this case, use database technology, the electronic version of an alphabetized shoebox, to get the same task done in much less time. The redeeming quality of the workaholic—and it is their saving grace—is that since they are motivated to succeed, all that they need to right their ship is training. This makes the workaholic an easy fix and is why I would rather have 10 of these individuals to work with than a single one of the next group— the dreaded "Spectators," which represent at least 50 percent of all salespeople, perhaps more.

The Spectators

Spectators, like their counterparts, the workaholics, have a significant asset in their favor: In this case, they are high on the "Knowledge" arm. They are well educated because they have been exposed to a lot of information. Unfortunately, in most cases the investment that is made in their education is by a third-party benefactor—specifically, their employer, acting as their rich uncle. They go to training programs because their boss makes them and because they are reimbursed for any and all associated costs. They have no "skin in the game," and therefore, the sense of urgency that you would expect a salesperson to demonstrate during training is replaced with a sense of entitlement.

What is the value of a spectator salesperson? Let me put it this way: If I were interviewing for a job opening, I would hire an untrained, inexperienced salesperson who is hungry for success over the most highly trained, field-experienced spectator I can find without hesitation every day of the week. I can teach a motivated person to be successful because that is the responsibility of the employer. I cannot teach an unmotivated person to want to be successful. Spectators therefore are well-educated people who are not motivated.

As far as training is concerned, I refer to this group as the "professional seminar attendees." They welcome every opportunity to attend training events; in fact, fully half of any audience will be comprised of these people. At these venues, their routine is always the same: They come in, get their donut (I find that this group favors the apple-cinnamon bear claw), pick up handout materials at the door, take a seat, and proceed to take it all in. They are attentive. They ask questions. They smile and nod; they take lots of notes. They buy books, audio CDs, and other learning products in the back of the room. Then, when they get back to the office, they sort through all the handouts, books, binders, CDs, DVDs, and whatever other booty they have acquired from the event, and place these items on a shelf in their office or cubicle. This is the designated place that they use to display their collection of knowledge for the world to see. The message to all the uneducated derelicts lurking around the office is obvious: "Look how much I know." There's just one small problem with this picture: The material is for display purposes only.

This is why these salespeople are spectators; they watch and wait for success to come and find them. They will do the easy part, which is to sit in a classroom or at a computer terminal and take a class ("Knowledge"), but they lack the motivation to have the follow-up commitment to implement the learning ("Application"). The workaholic has a skill problem that is easily correctable. The spectator's problem is one of motivation, which is not easily correctable. And, as the following example illustrates, the sales profession is not the only one that is infested with spectators.

Meet the Pros

I am fortunate to be a member of a superb organization called the *National Speakers Association* (NSA), which, as the name implies, is the industry trade association for my profession. NSA, like most groups with which I work as a speaker, has an annual conference at which members congregate to network, learn, stay up to date on industry trends and new developments, and enjoy themselves in the process. Our conference is always a well-attended event, with several thousand participants annually.

One of the most popular functions at the NSA convention is an event called "Meet the Pros." This special session allows up-and-coming speakers to sign up for a one-hour consultation with top performers—the "pros"—and, at a table with about 10 of their peers, ask questions of their pro regarding any number of topics on the business of being a professional speaker. Many celebrity-level pros, such as the great motivational speaker Zig Ziglar for one, are members of NSA and have served in this capacity, so the event is very popular with the attendees.

At my very first NSA convention, I learned that one of the pros who would be participating was Alan Weiss. Alan is an excellent writer; I had read several of his books and was a big fan. When I learned that Alan was going to be one of the hosts at Meet the Pros, I signed up immediately for his table and scored a coveted seat. I should note here that each pro conducts two sessions with about 10 participants each, so there were a total of 20 lucky "contestants" who got a seat at one of Alan's two programs, including me.

On the morning of the Meet the Pros sessions, when I arrived at Alan's table, though, all I found was note explaining that owing to a minor emergency, he would not be able to attend his own meeting. The note went on to say that since he had inconvenienced all 20 of us, he would offer, free of charge, a one-on-one coaching session with each person for a full half-hour on any issue that we needed help with in our speaking business. He provided a private e-mail address to contact him and set up an appointment.

I was suddenly very happy that he did not make his appearance that day.

As soon as the conference was over, I contacted Alan and made the following request regarding my half-hour allotment: I asked him to take 15 of my 30 minutes to read an outline I had prepared on the direction of my business and then use the remaining 15 minutes to give me some suggestions on how to accomplish those goals. He agreed to do this. My "free" session with him occurred nearly a decade ago, and I still use some of the ideas that he shared with me during that phone conference.

Remember that there were a total of 20 NSA members who were lucky enough to have been inconvenienced that day and were the recipients of this incredible opportunity. It is also worth mentioning that virtually all the members of the NSA are self-employed, so all our costs to attend the convention—airfare, hotel, meals, etc.—are out of pocket, to the tune of at least $1,000 per attendee. Therefore, this had to be a highly motivated group of 20 members, right? And when one of the most successful individuals in our profession offers a free one-on-one mentoring session, this lucky group of go-getters is going to be all over that offer, right?

The fact is that of the 20 people who were offered the free half-hour consultation with Alan Weiss, exactly two people took him up on it: myself and one other person. I learned this from Alan during our consult; when I asked him why this was the case, he made an astute observation: "Because 18 of the 20 people who were at my table that morning were there for one reason, and one reason only: so they could tell their friends, 'I sat at Alan Weiss's table for Meet the Pros!' and that is the sole reason that they took up a seat."

A few years later, I had my own Meet the Pros session, and I, too, had my 20 attendees split over two sessions. The program I presented, which was very well received, included a follow-up offer of a very useful item related to my topic that could be obtained only by contacting me via e-mail after the program.

Would you like to venture a guess as to how many of my speaker attendees followed up to take me up on the offer? Amazingly, the answer is two.

I shared this with Alan; and he made another astute observation: "You can always offer free items to your audiences because you will never have more than one or two people who will actually take you up on the offer."

In the time since then, I have found this always to be the case. Irrespective of the size of the group and the value of the offer, only a tiny fraction of the total audience actually will make the effort to obtain anything that must be proactively pursued following a program. The business world, and especially the field of sales, has an overabundance of spectators.

The Masters

If you add up the percentages from the whiners, workaholics, and spectators, you will find that you have, cumulatively, a total of 80 percent of all salespeople. This figure represents the bottom 80 percent per the Pareto principle—the same 80 percent who only produce 20 percent of the sales and get 20 percent of the benefit.

The "Masters" are those who now remain—the 20 percent of salespeople who get what every salesperson in the selling profession wants. What do these high achievers do that the others do not, and more important, why?

If you have been exposed to the marketing of any number of my peers, you doubtless have seen their claims that they will reveal to you the "Secrets of Success." This well-worn pitch is nothing but pure, unadulterated snake oil; there is no "secret" to being successful whatsoever. In fact, as the Mastery Grid shows, there are only two simple steps involved in being successful. In order, they are

- First, seek out information—educate yourself on better ways to do what you do every day as a salesperson.
- Second, when you find an idea that will improve your skill level, implement it—make it a part of who you are and what you do every day.

So there it is—the big "secret" to becoming a dominant predator. Learn first; then implement. This is all there is to it—it is what it is. This one habit is what separates the masters from the rest of the pack— in fact, it is the *only* thing. If you commit to the habit of education and implementation, it is impossible for you to *not* end up in the masters group—you will arrive there as surely as the sun rises in the morning.

Winning at competitive sales and being the best in your field is a very simple concept. Which begs the question: Why don't more salespeople make the commitment to high achievement? Why isn't everybody in the masters category? This is where things get more complicated.

An Offer You Can't Refuse
To answer this question, suppose that I were to make the following proposal to you: Implement the negotiating process outlined in Chapter 10. Learn it, practice it, and internalize it. Make it a part of you and therefore the way that you negotiate every business day. If you do this, I guarantee that you will *triple* your income next

year—and if you don't, I will personally give you the money that represents the shortfall between what you actually earn doing this and the money you need to triple your income. In other words, if you make the commitment to learn the material, you are guaranteed to triple your earnings next year.

Given those conditions, would you do it? Of course you would. You would do it because in that scenario there is no chance of failure; you are guaranteed success before you start. If only life—and success—worked that way. Since it doesn't—and since nothing that we attempt is guaranteed to be successful—most people are unwilling to make the leap from where they are to where they would like to be.

This is why there are so few people who really succeed in sales and so many people who really don't. This is why all salespeople exposed to the concepts in this chapter can clearly see the path to success but why so many of them cannot be persuaded to set their feet on it and get moving. They won't do it because it is not a sure thing. The issue is a lack of faith—they cannot bring themselves to believe in something that they have not yet experienced. Deep down inside, they doubt that if they were to do what I am describing—learn the negotiation process—they would receive the result that I am describing—triple their income. They say the idea may work for other people, but it won't work for them. They attend, and they sit. They listen, and they forget. They buy, and they shelve. They validate the old adage, "If you always do what you have already done, you will always get what you already have."

Is It In You?

So we now arrive at the point where you become the *decision maker*. The decision that you will now make is the level of success that you choose to attain in future competitive selling situations. Will you make the commitment to implement what you have learned? Will you master the steps in the competitive sale? Will you be one of the few salespeople who becomes a dominant predator? Or will you do what most salespeople might—put this book on a shelf and continue to struggle with competitive selling opportunities, just as you have done in the past? Market dominance or mediocrity—that is the choice that you are faced with, and it is yours alone to make.

Dominant predators will see this book for what it is—an important part of their continuing education. However, as we discussed earlier, simply becoming educated is not enough. Results come from the transfer of skills; meaning that to get real improvement, you must make a commitment to implement. You must make this competitive selling process a part of who you are, every day, in every competitive sale. This takes something that most people lack. It takes persistence.

For the last 25 years, this quote from Calvin Coolidge has been displayed on a plaque in my office. It is one of my personal favorites and timelessly summarizes this point:

> Nothing in the world can take the place of persistence. Talent will not;
> nothing is more common than unsuccessful men with talent. Genius
> will not; unrewarded genius is almost a proverb. Education will not;
> the world is full of educated derelicts. Persistence and determination
> alone are omnipotent.

In every market, in every business, there is one competitor who becomes the dominant predator. You have been provided with the tools that you need to join that elite group of salespeople. By making the commitment to become a dominant predator, you will take the step of implementing the strategies outlined in this book, and I will have accomplished my goal in writing it.

INDEX

Note: Boldface numbers indicate an illustration.

ABOUT THE AUTHOR

Landy Chase has worked with the sales forces of clients in over 60 different industries as a speaker, sales trainer, and advisor since founding his company, Landy Chase Incorporated, in 1993. His selling career included repeat President's Club awards as a salesperson, experience as a national sales trainer for a two-billion-dollar corporation, and field experience as a sales manager in both small-business and major-account business-to-business environments. He writes extensively as a columnist for a number of business publications and has published hundreds of articles on selling skills and sales management.

Chase is a graduate of The Citadel, the Military College of South Carolina, and holds an MBA from Xavier University in Cincinnati, Ohio. He holds the Certified Speaking Professional (CSP) designation from the National Speakers Association, the highest earned level of excellence in the speaking industry and a distinction representing the top 7 percent of all speakers worldwide. He and his family reside in the Charlotte, North Carolina area.

31901050787821